Happy Dog

Liz Dalby

INTERPET
PUBLISHING

Published in the UK in 2009 by
Interpet Publishing
Interpet House
Vincent Lane
Dorking
Surrey RH4 3YX

ISBN 978 1 8428 6204 9
QTT.HDO
A QUINTET BOOK

Conceived, designed and produced by
Quintet Publishing Limited
The Old Brewery
6 Blundell Street
London N7 9BH
United Kingdom

Designer: Ian Ascott
Art Director: Michael Charles
Managing Editor: Donna Gregory
Assistant Editor: Robert Davies
Publisher: James Tavendale

Colour separation in Singapore
Printed in China

9 8 7 6 5 4 3 2 1

CONTENTS

INTRODUCTION

Ever wanted to know how to interpret a dog's mood by its body language? How about training? Are you familiar with the one secret that ensures training success every time? If your dog is experiencing subclinical pain, would you even know it?

Happy Dog, a unique and informative guide that is sure to please even the most finicky dog fancier, has the answer to these and other questions related to our four-legged friends. Packed with colourful photographs and an abundance of helpful tips, *Happy Dog* offers an excellent overview of the basic fundamentals of dog ownership presented in a delightful, easy-to-read format. But don't be fooled. This book isn't just for beginners. Seasoned veterans can also benefit from the information contained within these pages, a handy refresher course that covers the key tenets of proper care for man's best friend.

Dog ownership is a big responsibility; one that should never be taken lightly. Our pets are wholly dependent upon on us for love, care and sustenance. In addition to obvious physical needs, including food, water, shelter and medical care, dogs require positive mental stimulation on a daily basis, as well as predictability and control in their lives blended with dependable social companionship. In return for these things, we are blessed with unconditional acceptance and affection, not to mention a tail that never fails to wag when we walk through that door, no matter how rough and tough our day has been.

It's a known fact among the veterinary community that dogs that are emotionally content generally suffer fewer health challenges (both psychological and physical) than do their emotionally-challenged peers. In other words, a happy dog is a healthy dog. Stress is bad, wreaking havoc on organ systems and increasing susceptibility to disease. That reality is true for us humans, and it's true for our four-legged friends as well. As a result, we need to make it our goal to minimize stress in the lives of our pets as much as we possibly can. How do we do this? Through proper husbandry practices, solid training and preventative health care.

If you are new to dogs, make it your mission to gather as much information about these and other subjects related to the species. Talk with your veterinarian, peruse the bookshelves, check out DVDs, surf the Net. Become an expert. Arm yourself with knowledge and the confidence that comes with that knowledge. By doing so, you'll be able to provide an exceptional quality of life for your dog, one of which you can be proud.

So get ready for an exciting journey. With *Happy Dog* as your guide, you're in for a treat.

Enjoy.

1 YOUR NEW DOG

Deciding to get a dog is a huge, life-changing decision. You need to be sure before you do it that you can offer a dog love, attention and care – 24 hours a day, seven days a week. Think: will you be prepared to train it, exercise it, feed it a good diet, play with it, groom it and look after its health? Not just when you feel like it, but all the time?

If you decide you are ready to take responsibility for a dog, then this book provides a starting point with some basic hints and tips that will help you to get the most out of the experience, and ensure that yours is a happy dog.

PUPPIES

If you have made the decision to get a dog, you have two choices: puppy or rescue. Looking after a puppy is hard work and time-intensive, but also fun and very rewarding. You'll need to commit yourself to training your new puppy, as well as providing it with constant company to help it settle into a new home away from its mother. Remember, too, that it won't stay a puppy forever – you need to be sure that you will be able to cope with it as an adult dog.

1

You will need to take the puppy outside very frequently to relieve itself until it is house-trained (see page 80). It will have accidents, though, so make sure you keep it in a place where this will not matter.

BUYING A PUPPY

When you buy a puppy, you should always ask to see the parents, or at least the mother. Not only does this give you an indication of the eventual size and temperament of the dog (this applies especially if it is mixed breed), but the puppy should not be taken away from its mother and litter before it is seven or eight weeks old.

Try to establish a routine to help your puppy feel secure. For example, try to feed it, play with it and exercise it at similar times each day. If you will need to leave it alone some of the time, build up to this gradually.

Make your home safe for the new puppy. Puppies will chew everything, including shoes, books, carpets and electrical cables. Ensure that anything dangerous or valuable is well out of the way.

RESCUE DOGS

You may choose to rehome a rescue dog instead of buying a puppy. Most of the dogs offered by rescue centres will be adults. The advantages of choosing an adult dog are that you know what you are getting in terms of size, and it will most likely be house-trained. However, you should always bear in mind that the dog was rescued for a reason and may have behavioural issues due to ill treatment in the past. Taking on a rescue dog is not an easy decision – you will need to be able to devote time to making it feel comfortable and able to trust you.

4

Don't expect to come back with a new dog on your first visit to a rescue centre. The staff will want to be sure that a dog is going to a home where it will feel secure and be cared for. Expect to answer plenty of questions and to receive a home visit. Remember, the better the match between you and your new dog in terms of temperament and energy levels, the more likely you are to be happy together.

WHEN NOT TO RESCUE

Centres should not allow you to rehome a rescue dog if you have young children (less than five years old). Also, you need to devote time to making the dog feel safe in its new home, so don't consider a rescue dog if you lead a very busy life.

5

Try to find out why the dog is being rehomed. It is quite likely to have been ill-treated or neglected in the past. If possible, try to observe the dog in a home environment before agreeing to take it. Behavioural issues may include aggression, barking and destructive tendencies. Ensure that you can return the dog if things don't work out, especially if you don't know its history.

READY FOR REHOMING

Rescue dogs should be in good general health, and should have been spayed or neutered (see page 114) before they are rehomed.

CHOOSING A PUPPY

There are two important decisions to make before choosing your puppy. First, you need to decide on the breed. Don't simply base your decision on looks – consider also the eventual size of the breed, its temperament and any hereditary diseases associated with it. Think realistically about how it would fit into your life. The second decision you need to make is the sex you would prefer. Male and female dogs have quite different characteristics. Be clear about these decisions before you start looking to avoid getting attached to a completely unsuitable puppy!

6

A purebred puppy will have parents of the same breed, making it possible to predict its eventual size. But purebred dogs are often susceptible to hereditary diseases. A vet or breeder will be able to advise you about specific examples. Ask to see results of health checks carried out on the parents.

7

Mixed breed puppies have parents of different breeds. It can be difficult to predict what size the adult dog will be, especially if you have not seen both parents.

MALE OR FEMALE?

Dogs (males) are generally more aggressive and highly sexed, more dominant and also more likely to wander off in search of females. Bitches (females) are gentler in temperament and easier to train, but can be moody when they are in heat. Unless you have your bitch spayed (see page 114), she is also at risk of becoming pregnant.

PERSONALITY

Don't choose the biggest or most aggressive puppy in a litter unless you definitely want a very lively alpha male. Also consider avoiding the smallest and most timid. Use your observations when you visit the litter, trust your instincts and ask the breeder about the characteristics of each puppy.

8

For any puppy, try to find out as much as you can about the temperament of the parents to give you an indication of the behaviour to expect.

BRINGING YOUR PUPPY HOME

Before bringing your puppy home, you should make some basic preparations. The way you treat the puppy from the start may affect its behaviour for the rest of its life, so it is important to get the details right. You need to devote time and care to making the puppy's transition from the litter to the wider world as stress-free as possible.

THE JOURNEY HOME

You'll need to bring the puppy home in the car – it can't walk around outside of your home and garden until it's been vaccinated (see page 16). Make sure the puppy has relieved itself before you start off. For this first journey, someone (not the driver) should hold the puppy in an old towel or blanket, and talk to it gently to reassure it.

9

You'll need the following equipment before you bring your puppy home for the first time: a dedicated space for the puppy (this could be a room, cage or crate); food and water bowls; toys and things to chew; a collar and lead; dry puppy food... and plenty of newspaper!

10

Try to be with your puppy as much as possible for the first few days. Make time to feed it three or four times a day as this is what it will have been used to. Avoid disrupting its routine too much at first – it will have been through a lot of upheaval already.

IDENTIFICATION

Get your new puppy used to wearing a collar with an identity disc inscribed with its name and your telephone number. Consider getting a microchip fitted; this will increase the chances of your dog being returned to you if it is lost.

11

To make the puppy feel more at home right away, ask the breeder if you can bring an object containing the scent of the puppy's mother and the littermates – such as a blanket – back to your home.

THE FIRST FEW MONTHS

Your new puppy will need some special treatment to keep it happy and healthy in the first few months of its life. First, it will need a general health check and vaccination. It may pick up parasites and infections, which you should be aware of. The dietary requirements of puppies are also slightly different from those of adult dogs.

12

A two-month-old puppy needs four or five small meals per day; a four-month-old puppy needs three meals per day, while a one-year-old dog needs only one or two meals a day. Feed a young puppy small meals to avoid stretching its stomach.

VACCINATION

When your puppy is around eight weeks old, you should take it to the vet. The vet will check its general health and can also advise you about any hereditary diseases to be aware of. The vet may also give the puppy its first vaccination at that time. A week after the first vaccination, the puppy can mix with other dogs and humans. Once it has had its follow-up booster vaccinations it is free from the risk of certain dangerous diseases.

13

As well as food, it is important that your puppy always has access to fresh drinking water.

TEETH

Puppies get their first milk teeth at two weeks old. By eight weeks, they have around 28 teeth, though no molars. At four to six months old, the permanent teeth come through. At this time, the puppy may have sore gums and want to chew things. The puppy will end up with 42 permanent teeth. If any milk teeth remain, they may need to be removed by the vet.

HYGIENE

Puppies are susceptible to parasites such as fleas and worms. You should always treat these as they can be detrimental to the puppy's health. Puppies may also experience diarrhoea, which may be caused by overfeeding, stress, intestinal parasites or bacterial infection. To avoid picking up any infection yourself, always wash your hands after handling the puppy.

14

If for any reason you make changes to the puppy's diet, introduce them gradually over the course of a week to avoid upsetting healthy digestion.

SOCIALIZATION

Socialization is the vitally important process by which your puppy becomes familiar with other animals and people. It also needs to learn to cope with the stimuli in its immediate environment, such as cars and other loud noises. Socialization needs to take place when the puppy is between three and 14 weeks old – a time known as the "sensitive period". A puppy that is not exposed to other animals may become fearful and aggressive towards them.

15

Your vet or local training centre may organize "puppy parties". Take your puppy along to one to give it the chance to interact with other dogs in a safe and controlled environment.

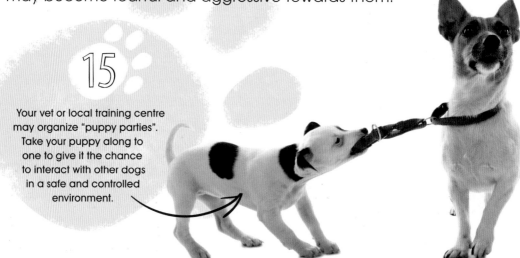

16

Once your puppy has received all its vaccinations, take it out of the house frequently so it can meet lots of new people and other dogs. It will also become used to traffic.

OVER-DEPENDENCY

While it is important that you spend plenty of time with your puppy, it does need to get used to being on its own as well. A dog that is constantly with its owner can become over-dependent and unhappy when left alone for any period of time. If the puppy is trained to accept solitude, this will prevent it from developing separation anxiety (see page 26).

BEDTIME

You shouldn't let your puppy sleep with you for two main reasons: it needs to respect you as the dominant one in the relationship; and it may have parasites which could get onto your bedding. So it should have its own bed, made of sturdy, unchewable plastic. The bed becomes the puppy's own space where it can feel safe and secure. You can place the bed near your own to start with, if you like, and then gradually move it away as the puppy's confidence grows.

17

If you get into the habit of checking your puppy's ears, teeth and feet on a daily basis, it will become used to being examined and will be less likely to be scared of a trip to the vet.

2 BEHAVIOUR

A dog may be "man's best friend", but it functions in quite a different way from a human. It's important to understand why your dog does the things it does, be it jumping up to greet visitors, smelling every dog it encounters, wagging its tail, refusing to get into your car, growling at "intruders" or simply barking incessantly. Only then can you take steps to avert or correct any behavioural problems.

The way your dog behaves is governed by many factors. It may act out of boredom, or due to a built-in instinct. Some types of behaviour are age-related; the things it does when it is a puppy will not necessarily persist into its adult life. The dog's breed will also have a bearing on its tendency to behave in a particular way, such as whether it is likely to become frustrated by a lack of exercise or to develop dominant or submissive tendencies.

BARKING AND HOWLING

Dogs bark for several different reasons. They may bark to greet someone they know, as a request to play or simply to seek attention. A bark can also be used to threaten other dogs or people, or to call for company. A howl is an extreme distress call – usually used by a dog who feels scared. Barking and howling can become unacceptable, but it is possible to train your dog to bark on demand – and then to be quiet.

GETTING A RESPONSE

Barking for attention is often a successful form of behaviour for a dog, simply because it usually results in you responding in some way – by telling the dog to be quiet, for instance, or distracting it with toys or food.

18

A well-exercised, happy dog that is not left alone for long periods of time is less likely to bark incessantly than one that is bored or frustrated.

BARKING AT "INTRUDERS"

Many dogs are frightened of potential "intruders". Again, barking is a successful reponse to this kind of situation. Often people who approach your house, such as the postman, will simply go away again anyway (once the post is delivered). But your dog will perceive that its barking drove the intruder away.

19

Don't shout at your dog to try to stop its barking. It will just think you are joining in and will bark even more!

CONTROLLING BARKING

Barking is natural behaviour for a dog, and you can't – and shouldn't – prevent it entirely. But excessive barking can be unacceptable, and it is possible to train your dog to bark and be quiet on demand. When your dog is barking, ignore it. Any kind of attention could be interpreted as praise. When your dog starts to bark, say "bark!" and offer a reward. When the dog has been barking for several seconds, say "quiet", and give it the reward. The dog will have to stop barking once it takes the reward in its mouth.

AGGRESSION

Dogs show signs of aggression for various reasons. An aggressive dog is often nervous or scared, or it may show signs of territorial aggression or it could simply be frustrated. Dogs can be aggressive towards other dogs or humans. It is important to deal with signs of aggressive behaviour to keep your dog from attacking other animals or people. Most dog attacks on humans are directed towards family members, friends or other people known to the dog – often children.

FEAR OR NERVOUS AGGRESSION

Fear is a common cause of aggression in dogs. It may be a trait inherited from the mother, so check for this characteristic when you buy the puppy. Another cause of nervousness is a lack of early socialization (see page 18). If you are nervous around dogs, your dog may pick up on this, causing it to become fearful and aggressive when you are out walking. It may also show aggression towards humans if it wasn't handled enough as a puppy.

GROWLING

A growl is generally a warning, meaning "leave me alone". It can be a sign that the dog is anxious. A dog on a lead that feels threatened (because it can't escape) may growl. Growling, for example when playing, can instil fear in the dog's owner, and a dog may learn to use this to get its own way.

20

If a dog suddenly becomes aggressive, there may be a medical reason, such as epilepsy, diabetes, pain or thyroid dysfunction. Consult your vet if you think this is the case.

21

Some dogs display "territorial" aggression towards other dogs (and humans) when on home ground, but are not bothered by them on neutral territory.

22

If a dog is not allowed to interact with other dogs or humans, it may show aggression out of frustration.

CURING AGGRESSION

Aggression can be cured, but it takes time. Give your dog gentle, repeated exposure to the thing it fears. Don't shout at the dog when it shows signs of aggression, but don't reassure it either (which encourages it). Try to remain calm and relaxed. Neutering may also help with aggression.

SEPARATION ANXIETY

Most dogs – especially if you obtain them as puppies – will acclimatize to your lifestyle quickly and easily. But not all dogs find it so easy to adapt to a new home, something which is particularly true of rescue dogs.

The anxiety they feel when separated from familiar surroundings can cause some of the most costly behavioural problems of all: it may necessitate repairs to damaged furniture, rebuilding friendships with irritated neighbours and even paying fines if your dog's frustration leads to you making an appearance in court.

WHAT CAUSES IT?

Dogs are inherently pack animals. They live and function best in the constant environment of a familiar group. The domestic dog adopts its owners as a substitute pack – and unfortunately the reality is that we often need to leave the dog alone while we go to work or school, do the shopping, or enjoy an evening out. Many dogs find it difficult to adjust to being on their own for so much of the time. If the dog has previously had a frightening experience when left alone in the house – a storm or a break-in, for example – then it is likely to be anxious at the thought of being separated from its owners in the future.

23

Try to set up audiovisual recording equipment to see what happens when you're away from home. You might find there are specific triggers to your dog's anxiety that you can help to prevent in future.

SYMPTOMS

Dogs experiencing separation anxiety commonly display displacement behaviours arising from their anxiety. They may chew furniture, scratch doors and try to dig into the ground in an effort to distract themselves. Many dogs will also bark and howl shortly after their owner leaves the house, trying to call back other members of the "pack" – the owners – and dogs often soil the house from fear.

PROBLEM DOGS

Your vet may choose to support behavioural therapy with drugs to help calm very anxious dogs. You may consider placing a DAP diffuser in the room where the dog is to be left. These appliances emit calming pheromones into the air, but they have a limited area capacity, so this may not work if the dog is to be left in a very large space. Never use indoor kennels or cages to contain anxious dogs, as this will only add to their frustration and could lead to further psychological damage.

24

When desensitizing the dog to the sound of the door being opened or closed, do it loudly each time and let the dog see you are still there. This will ensure the dog does not associate these sounds with you actually leaving.

BODY LANGUAGE

Though dogs may make noises, they can't speak as we do, so body language is a vital layer of communication for them. They use all the parts of the body to communicate, but especially the ears, eyes, mouth, tail and torso. Perhaps the most important part, in terms of body language, is the tail. Observe your dog's body language to try to understand it better, but bear in mind that it can be open to misinterpretation.

MOOD INDICATORS

The following is a guide to some of your dog's moods:

Alert: pricked ears, upright stance
About to attack: ears back, teeth bared, aggressive stance with "hackles" raised
Confident: tail up, upright stance
Frightened: tail between legs, back end lowered, whites of eyes showing
Happy: ears back, eyes half closed, wagging tail
Submissive: ears back, rolling on back, exposing tummy

25

Eye contact is important to dogs. A dominant dog may glare at a lower-ranking dog (see page 40) or else give it a look of approval. The way you look at dogs is important, too. They will learn to interpret the looks you give them.

26

One expressive posture you will want to learn to recognize is the invitation to play – with the front legs lowered, the bottom high in the air, ears up and mouth open in eager anticipation!

SIGNS OF AGGRESSION

An aggressive dog will exhibit particular body language. This may include a sturdy standing posture, with the hairs around the neck and along the back (the "hackles") raised, the lips drawn back and the tail held out straight. But bear in mind these signs may be difficult to spot (or entirely different) in different breeds.

VOCALIZATION

Of course, not all dog communcation is by silent gesture. Dogs whine, bark and growl as well (see page 24). Growling, in particular, can have a range of meanings, from an expression of pleasure to an extreme threat of aggression. Some dogs even seem to "talk" to their owners for minutes at a time. While neither side may understand what is being "said", this method of communication is important to the dog because it elicits a response.

SENSE OF SMELL

Smell is probably a dog's most important sense, offering it vital clues about its immediate environment. Puppies rely on their sense of smell almost immediately to locate their initial food source – their mother's milk – as they can't see for several weeks after being born. Even in adult dogs, the sense of sight is not as accurate as in humans, and so they, too, rely heavily on their sense of smell, along with hearing.

INFORMATION FROM SCENT

When dogs encounter each other, you will notice that they spend a long time sniffing each other, paying special attention to the rear ends. This is because the scents given off by other dogs' urine, faeces, anal sacs, vaginas and the glands around their necks and bottoms convey essential information.

URINE MARKING

In the wild, dogs urinate in prominent places to mark the boundaries of their territory. In domestic dogs, this translates to an urge to urinate on streetlamps, trees and so on – marking out the boundaries of what they think of as their territory. Bitches will also urinate to convey information about their sexual availability when they are in heat.

EXCESSIVE URINATION

Excessive urination may be due to a behavioural problem if it happens in the home – a dominant dog may scent-mark; a submissive dog may urinate out of fear. The root causes of both problems need addressing, rather than just the issue of urination. When out walking, your dog may want to urinate every few minutes, which can ruin the walk and result in a lack of exercise. Try to discourage your dog from doing this by walking on and not allowing it to stop and investigate every smell – use a toy or treat as a distraction if the problem is very bad.

27

Dogs have such a highly developed sense of smell that some can be trained as sniffer dogs, and used to detect bombs in luggage, or drugs being smuggled across borders.

NERVOUSNESS

Dogs can be nervous for a variety of reasons. Your dog may naturally have a nervous disposition, or it may be nervous of a specific thing or situation. Common causes of nervousness in dogs include fear of loud sounds, such as traffic, fireworks or thunderstorms; other dogs or people; physical abuse; or a reaction to a particular diet. There are ways to help your dog overcome its nervousness – and good reasons why you should – but they will take time and patience.

NERVOUS BREEDS

Some breeds are naturally more nervous than others. Examples of highly strung breeds include border collies, some terriers, chihuahuas, greyhounds, whippets, Dobermans and pointers. The problem can also affect mixed breeds, especially if one or both of the parents are from a breed predisposed to nervousness. You should take this into account, especially if you have children; in this case, consider choosing a sturdy, placid breed, such as a retriever or standard poodle.

28

For a nervous dog, the instinctive reactions are flight or fight. This is why a dog that feels cornered may snap or bite.

29

Don't reassure your dog when it's showing signs of fear – this will reinforce the behaviour. Instead, try giving it something else to think about, by playing with it or distracting it with food.

30

Your dog's diet may make a difference to how nervous it is. Foods high in cereal or sugar can exacerbate anxiety.

31

Some dogs' nervousness may be caused by a lack of vitamin B6. You could try giving your dog a supplement, but consult your vet first.

EXTERNAL CAUSES

If your dog has ever suffered physical abuse or neglect, or if it was a stray, it may be prone to nervousness. This is especially likely to apply if you choose to rehome a rescue dog. Choose a rescue dog carefully and observe it in a home environment first if possible. You should never physically abuse a dog or shout at it to discipline it. Lack of exercise can also cause anxiety – especially in active breeds such as pointers – so make sure to exercise your dog every day.

NATURAL INSTINCTS

Pet dogs retain some deep-rooted natural instincts, including digging, burying things, making dens and chasing. It may help to understand the origins of these behavioural traits in order to be able to train them to respond to you and curb their instincts when you want them to.

BURYING

In the wild, a dog may kill an animal that is too big to eat at once, so it will bury it to preserve it. Domestic dogs have the urge to bury bones and other prizes to prevent them from being taken. Unlike dogs in the wild, pet dogs are likely to forget what they have buried as they have no real need for it (in the wild they would have to return to find it or else go hungry).

DIGGING

Some breeds of dogs dig in order to catch animals such as badgers, foxes and otters. If you have a breed prone to this – such as a terrier or a dachshund – you could provide it with a special place to dig, such as a sandpit, to prevent it from digging up your garden. Often dogs dig simply because they are bored, so provide them with diversions, or play with them to distract them. The urge to escape from your garden – especially to try to mate with another dog – may also prompt digging.

32

The chase instinct is strong in some dogs. It can be annoying if it causes your dog to run away and not come back. Train the dog to respond to a recall signal (see page 52) and always reward it when it finally returns.

DENNING

The "denning" instinct may be strong in your dog – the need for a safe and secure place can cause it to hide out under furniture, in a hole in the garden, in its kennel or in a cage. Contrary to what you might think, leaving your dog in a cage when you go out can be quite comforting for it. It also safeguards against the dog trashing your house in your absence.

33

Taking an item – such as a shoe – and running off with it is attention-seeking behaviour. The best way to deal with this is simply to ignore it.

JUMPING UP

Many dogs "jump up" to greet people coming into your house. Jumping up, sometimes accompanied by barking, is essentially friendly behaviour, but it can be off-putting and intimidating for your visitors, especially if the dog is large or the visitors are small or frail. This makes it unacceptable behaviour.

DOMINANT BEHAVIOUR

Jumping up to greet visitors can be a sign that your dog feels dominant. This is probably a sign that you need to be more controlling in general. Some dogs are perfectly well aware of their place in the pack, but jump at visitors as a way of alerting their leaders (you) to possible danger in the form of an intruder.

34

A dog that jumps up at people will tend to aim for the mouth area. Any kind of response – trying to push the dog away, or reciprocal affection – will encourage the dog to repeat the behaviour to get a reaction.

WANTING TO PLAY

Some dogs jump up to seek attention, for example if they want to play. This can be a sign that the dog needs more stimulation, either from you playing with it or by providing it more toys and chews for it to amuse itself with when you are not around. However, responding directly to the demand will only encourage the jumping up behaviour. When the dog has been good, and not jumped up recently, reward it by playing with it.

35

Rescue dogs may be particularly bad jumpers – some will have been badly trained and may even have been encouraged to jump up in the past.

36

Try greeting the dog in a crouched position to discourage jumping up.

TRAINING THE DOG NOT TO JUMP

The best way to teach a dog not to jump up is to instil in it that it will not receive any attention until it sits. Every time you arrive home, tell the dog to sit. Ignore it completely until it does sit, then praise it calmly. Or give it a treat. You will need to ask all visitors to your house to adopt the same approach, and give them a treat to give to the dog. If this technique fails, use the lead to control the dog's behaviour – insist that the dog sits and stays as visitors are brought in.

CHEWING

Chewing usually starts when a puppy loses its milk teeth, between three and seven months old. The puppy chews to alleviate the pain in its gums and to speed up the process of the milk teeth falling out. Chewing may persist in the form of "adolescent" exploratory chewing – from around seven to twelve months of age. This is often a result of gum discomfort as the adult teeth settle into the young dog's mouth, or as a way of finding out about its environment.

POSITIVE CHEWING

Chewing is perfectly natural behaviour, but you do need to teach your dog the difference between things that it can chew and things that it shouldn't. Supply your dog with things that are safe to chew and will not splinter – such as dog chews and toys – as this may help to reduce the incidence of the dog chewing things that are not acceptable, such as doors.

37

You can buy sprays that act as chewing deterrents by making an object taste unpleasant. However, these only work for a very short period of time.

CORRECTING MISTAKES

Reward your dog for chewing the right things, but correct it if it is about to chew the wrong thing. Use a short squirt from a water pistol to startle it, as soon as it begins to chew. If you are too late – and the dog has already started chewing – distract it by calling it or showing its lead.

BOREDOM AND DISTRESS

Some dogs chew out of boredom or frustration. Boredom is likely to affect working dogs, such as springer spaniels, in particular. Exercise your dog regularly and play with it for short bursts several times a day. Some dogs feel distress at being left alone (see page 26), and this can result in destructive tendencies. Consider leaving your dog in a cage when you go out to keep it from chewing household items. Don't leave it unsupervised near dangerous or valuable things.

38

Some dogs like to chew on stones and plaster. This could be a sign of calcium deficiency in the diet. If you suspect this, consult the vet for dietary advice.

39

Remember – chewing is not the dog's fault and isn't done to wind you up – it's most likely a response to painful gums, or boredom.

40

Give your dog a chew at a time when you want it to settle down; perhaps when you go out. Adult dogs need to chew too, and chewing helps keep their teeth clean.

PACK MENTALITY

In the wild, dogs live in packs. In this way they receive the support and protection of other dogs. Pet dogs do not live in packs, but still possess "pack mentality", and consider the family and other animals they live with to be their pack. You need to establish the human occupants of your home as the pack leaders, dominant to the dog or dogs. This is important not only to help you train the dog to behave in a socially acceptable and safe way, but also to help it feel secure.

DOMINANT DOGS

A dominant dog considers itself superior to some or all of the human members of the household. This is a problem because the dog will be difficult to train, and as a result, may behave in unacceptable or even dangerous ways. A dominant dog is likely to be untrustworthy around children and, in extreme cases, may have to be euthanized.

If the dog is in your way – lying in a doorway, for example – make it move rather than stepping over or around it. If you are both walking through the same doorway, you should always go first.

SUBMISSIVE DOGS

Just as some dogs consider themselves dominant within the "pack", others are overly submissive. For a dog in the home, this tends to translate into a desire to lick people's faces and hands. Although it is not "bad" behaviour, you should discourage it for hygiene reasons. Try to discourage face-licking gently, though, because the dog is already submissive, and you do not want to make this worse.

Don't let your dog sit in people's laps or on the furniture. To reinforce the message that you are the dominant one in the relationship, though, you should sometimes go and sit in the dog's bed.

Only let your dog eat after you have eaten, and never feed it food from your plate.

Play with your dog, but on your terms. You should initiate games, not the other way around.

TRAVEL SICKNESS

Travel sickness in dogs is most often caused by stress from fear or excitement, though it may also be due to the motion of the car, which affects the dog's inner ear in the same way that it does in some humans. Your puppy's first car journey is likely to have been the one that took it away from the litter and its mother, which may be one reason that dogs come to associate travelling by car with unpleasant experiences. It is possible to accustom a travel-sick dog to making fuss-free journeys, but as with all aspects of training, this will take time and patience.

POSITIVE EXPERIENCES

Start training your dog to manage car journeys when it is a puppy. Try to teach your dog to associate car journeys with something pleasant – a trip to the park or the beach, for example. Build up to making longer journeys gradually; first of all, simply acclimatize your dog to being in the car without moving, then try very short journeys with a positive experience awaiting it at the end.

MINIMIZING RISK

When you travel with your dog, you can minimize the risk of travel sickness by taking a few simple precautions. Limit the amount of water your dog drinks before a journey, and avoid feeding it for three or four hours before you travel. This makes vomiting much less likely. Allowing the dog to roam around the car or look out of the window can make motion sickness worse, so hold the dog securely or put it in a crate or cage. Make sure the car is well ventilated, and on a long journey, make plenty of rest stops, taking the dog out of the car each time.

45

Tempt a reluctant dog into a car with a tidbit and reward with praise once it is in.

46

Many puppies outgrow their travel sickness when they are a year old. If the sickness persists, consult the vet, who may be able to prescribe helpful medication.

47

Never leave your dog inside a parked car. It may overheat, become dehydrated and could even die.

INTRODUCING A NEW BABY

Meeting your new baby can be stressful for your dog. The dog needs to understand that the baby is a new member of the pack so the two can begin to form a bond. It is vital that your dog is obedience-trained before you bring the baby into your home. You need to be able to trust the dog to sit, stay and not to get overexcited around the child.

BEFORE BABY ARRIVES

Give your dog "practice" in dealing with a baby – make it sit and stay while you attend to a doll wrapped in a blanket, for example. Praise and reward the dog for staying still. Get the dog used to recorded baby sounds such as crying. Introduce your dog to as many real babies as possible to accustom it to their distinct look, smell, sound and way of moving. Offer your dog treats whenever it is near a baby to reinforce positive associations. Over time, start to reduce the amount of attention you give your dog.

BRINGING BABY HOME

A day or two before the baby arrives home, bring a blanket back from the hospital for the dog to smell – and as it does so, give it treats. (Don't allow the dog to play with the blanket.) When mother and baby first arrive home, get someone else to hold the baby while the mother reintroduces herself to the dog. Gradually bring the dog nearer to the baby, on a lead and wearing a muzzle if you are at all worried that it may snap. Allow the dog to sniff the baby and get used to it.

LIVING TOGETHER

Never allow the dog to be with the baby unsupervised. Take special care when the baby is crying or waving its arms and legs, as this may excite your dog. To alleviate any jealousy, allow the dog to be near when you are with the baby – make it sit and stay and reward good behaviour with praise and tidbits so it associates the baby with positive things.

48

Never leave your dog alone or unsupervised with a baby or small child, no matter how uninterested it appears to be.

49

Don't exclude your dog after the arrival of a new baby.

50

Although you need to be aware of the danger your dog could pose to your baby, remember that most dogs adjust to babies perfectly happily.

TODDLERS AND DOGS

Once your toddler starts moving around, it will interact with the dog in ways that could annoy or confuse the dog – pulling its tail, hugging it, pinching it and so on. Pre-empt any adverse reaction from your dog by doing these things yourself, and giving treats at the same time; the dog will get used to being treated in slightly unexpected ways.

INTRODUCING A NEW ANIMAL

Whether you are bringing a new dog into a home where there is an older dog or cat, or introducing a new kitten to a home in which your dog is already established, you need to follow a few simple rules to help the process go smoothly. Remember that the original animal needs to feel included and not starved of attention, however fascinating a new young puppy or kitten may be.

NEW DOG ON THE BLOCK

An older dog may find it hard to accept the arrival of a new puppy in your home. It inevitably means that there will be less attention to go around, and it will have to get used to sharing its space. The puppy will, of course, be completely oblivious to this, and may try to greet the older dog boisterously, biting and tugging at it in an attempt to initiate a game. This could be annoying for the older dog and, unless it is extremely placid, it is likely to warn the puppy off with a growl or even a nip. Try to arrange the introduction so that it happens in the garden in case things get a little heated.

51
If you have more than one dog, provide them each with a house cage to allow them a place where they can be on their own if they want to. This is also important if you leave them alone often.

52
Stand up for your older dog – don't allow a new arrival to take its toys or food.

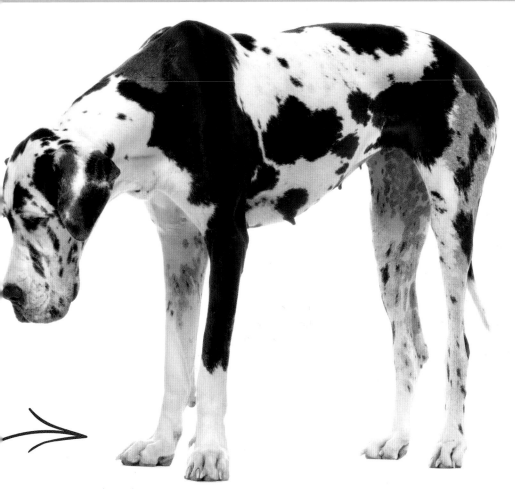

DOGS AND CATS

Dogs and cats are traditionally viewed as enemies. If you bring a new puppy into a home where there is already a cat, you need to train the dog to respect the cat from the start, for the safety and well-being of both animals. The first hurdle to overcome is getting them used to each other. To achieve this, simply place one of them in a crate or cage but allow them to occupy the same space so that each gets used to the way the other smells and looks. Gradually, allow them to interact. They should start to tolerate each other and may even surprise you by becoming friends. However, some cats and dogs never get along.

3 EXERCISE

Daily exercise is essential to your dog's well-being. Not only does it get a cardiovascular workout, but it will develop stamina and build up muscle tone. A well-exercised dog is also much more likely to be happy and less prone to behavioural problems than one that is shut up inside for long stretches. You need to consider whether you can commit to walking a dog every day before you get one, bearing in mind that big dogs will need much more exercise than small ones, and that certain breeds are also more demanding.

The main form of exercise is walking. Before you go walking there are some things you need to consider, including your responsibilities to the other people and animals you are likely to encounter along the way. Your dog should have had some basic obedience training at least, and you should also keep it on a lead in built-up areas or around farm and wild animals. Aside from walking, there are other excellent forms of exercise you may not have thought of, including swimming and agility training. Agility training can be tremendous fun for you and your dog, and you can take it as seriously as you choose to – there are even opportunities to compete at an international level if it goes well.

WALKING

Walking your dog every day is essential – not only for its health and general well-being but also to prevent any behavioural problems associated with frustration. In built-up areas and public parks, it is likely that you will need to keep your dog on a lead (this may be a legal requirement), but sometimes you will want to let your dog off the lead, in which case it is useful if it is trained to walk "to heel".

WEARING A COLLAR AND LEAD

A collar with an identity tag is a legal requirement, so your dog will need to wear one from an early age. Introduce the collar for short periods at first and build up to wearing it all the time. Once it is used to the collar, introduce the lead. Train the dog to walk around the garden wearing the collar and lead initially, before venturing into the wider world.

WALKING TO HEEL

Start training your dog to walk to heel in your garden. Walk around the garden with a treat visible in your hand to encourage your dog walk beside you. As the dog follows you, say "heel", and give the dog treats at intervals. Once the dog is good at doing this, hide the treats, but continue to reward the dog for walking to heel. Build up gradually to practising the exercise outside the garden, with the dog on a lead. Eventually you should be able to let the dog off the lead but have it walking to heel on your command.

53

When you are training your dog to walk to heel, don't spend too long doing it at any one time as it can be very boring for the dog. Short, sharp bursts of training are more effective.

54

Dogs pull on the lead either to reach something they are interested in more quickly, or to signify that they are in charge of the pace and direction of the walk.

TYPES OF LEADS

Leads come in a variety of forms. Most leads attach to the collar, though some attach to harnesses – these may help to control pulling on the lead. There are also extendable and retractable versions that allow the dog some freedom. Some people use chain choke collars to help them control their dogs – these tighten around the neck if the dog pulls too vigorously. However, they can damage the dog's trachea if they are overused.

RECALL

Recall training means teaching the dog to come to you on command – it's essential in order to be able to let your dog off the lead with confidence. You need to be sure that you can call your dog back to you – and that it will come – to protect it from potentially dangerous situations.

STARTING RECALL TRAINING

Start recall training with a puppy – it will have a strong urge to return to its mother and will transfer this urge to you with a little encouragement. Choose a word for the recall command – don't simply use the dog's name. The dog will be used to hearing its name in a whole range of situations, and it will be too confusing for it to associate it with a particular command. Use a short, simple command, such as "come".

SUCCESSFUL RECALL

Once you start recall training, whenever the dog comes towards you, say "come" (or whatever command word you are using). However, don't keep repeating "come" if the dog is not coming towards you, or it will infer that it's all right to ignore the command. You need to aim for a successful recall every time.

55

The best time to start recall training is when your dog is hungry; food is an excellent incentive. Treat the dog when it comes to you, and offer lots of praise and affection.

56

Start recall training on the lead (consider using an extendable one) and gradually build up to letting the dog off the lead once you are confident it will come when called.

NEGATIVE ASSOCIATIONS

When you are training your dog to come at recall, it's very important that the experience of responding to the recall is always positive. Never recall your dog and then tell it off for any reason. If you need to reprimand the dog, then go to it; don't call it to you. Likewise, don't only recall your dog when it's time to go home at the end of a walk, or when you are going out and you need to shut it inside. The dog will start to associate the recall command with things it doesn't want to do, and stop responding.

WALK PRACTICALITIES

Your dog is raring to go for a walk, but there are some essential things you need to bear in mind before you set off, such as where to walk, consideration for the people and animals you might meet along the way, cleaning up after your dog and even what to do in the terrible event that you lose your dog.

58

Be sensitive to wildlife and farm animals; birds in particular may be scared away from places where people walk their dogs frequently. Don't let your dog off the lead near farm animals.

57

Try researching places to walk on the Internet, or in walking magazines – keep it interesting for you as well as your dog! The more you enjoy the walking, the less likely you are to find excuses not to go.

59

Always carry a "poop scoop" or some bags to pick up your dog's faeces, and dispose of them in a designated bin. In most places, it's against the law to let your dog foul a public area.

60

If you're going on a long walk, take enough water for your dog. Take a paper cup or an inflatable dish for it to drink from.

EXERCISING PUPPIES

Puppies don't need as much exercise as adult dogs; too much walking can damage their joints, and they may develop arthritis when they are older. A good rule to follow is five minutes per month of age, twice a day. Once the dog is fully grown, you can of course take it on much longer walks.

LOST!

If the worst happens and you lose your dog while you are out, search the area immediately. Give your contact details and a description of your dog to anyone you meet. Call your vet and the police station. If your dog is microchipped, alert the tracking company. In the longer term, make posters and flyers with the dog's name, a recent photo and your details, and distribute them in the area in which the dog was lost.

Lost Dog

Samson
Male Border Collie
Last Seen in sports field on 9th January
If you have seen him or know where
he is call me URGENTLY
t: 0380 0893939
Reward

TAKE A BREAK

If it's hot, let your dog rest every so often in a shady spot. Dogs can't sweat like we do – they cool down by panting. If there is a clean river or stream, you could let the dog go for a swim. If your dog is unwell, old or obese, don't take it on a longer walk than it can manage. Check with the vet if you are unsure. Build up gradually to longer distances.

GARDEN EXERCISE

Walking is an important form of exercise, but your dog also needs somewhere safe where it can go for fresh air, to relieve itself or to play on its own or with you. Letting your dog run around a garden does not provide it with all the exercise it needs – you need to walk it too – but it can be valuable as part of a larger exercise regime and is important for the dog's general well-being.

JUST CHILLING

Most of the time your dog is in the garden, it won't be exercising much. If you watch what it does, you will see it strolling around, resting in the shade, watching things go by and generally chilling out. It will rarely move around fast enough to get any kind of cardiovascular workout, which is why you need to walk it every day as well.

61

Never leave your dog unattended in your garden when you go out. It may escape or could even be stolen.

62

Provide a place to dig if your dog enjoys digging (see page 34). Make a sandpit so the dog can see where to dig – place it in the shade as this is where your dog will instinctively prefer to dig.

63

Playing with your dog helps to alleviate any boredom it may feel. It also provides it with more exercise than simply walking or running around the garden. Aim for 15 to 20 minutes of play every day (see page 92).

GARDEN DANGERS

You may think it's quite safe to just let your dog out into the garden, but do check that it's "dogproof" before you do. Problems may arise, especially when your dog goes through the chewing stage (see page 38) and will have a go at eating almost anything. Possible dangers to watch out for include fertilizers, poisonous bugs and snakes, poisonous plants and swimming pool supplies.

64

Dogs like to watch the world go by – try to arrange a place where yours can see things from, such as a raised mound.

SWIMMING

Most dogs love to splash around and swim in muddy streams and puddles. It's great fun for them, but swimming can also have health benefits; it improves fitness, stamina and also muscle tone. Swimming uses all the muscles that other forms of exercise do but with less stress on the bones and joints. As long as you follow a few basic safety guidelines, it should be quite safe to let your dog dive in.

LEARNING TO SWIM

Dogs have a natural instinct to paddle, but that does not mean that all dogs can swim, or that they will stay afloat for very long. Start off teaching your dog to swim in shallow water. Don't venture into deep water until you are sure that the dog will come back when you call it (see page 52). It may help your dog learn to swim if you take along another, more experienced dog to show it.

65

Never, under any circumstances, let your dog swim alone. Watch to make sure that it does not go too far out into deep water.

CONVALESCENT DOGS

Swimming can be a good, gentle form of exercise for overweight dogs (see page 70). It can help a dog recuperate after an injury or operation – it is especially good for helping to counteract the effects of muscle wastage, which starts to happen after just a few days of inactivity. You can even take your dog to a special spa or hydrotherapy pool. Here, the water will be heated, and you may even be encouraged to get in and help your dog to move around if need be.

66

Don't throw an object to be retrieved too far; the dog may get tired trying to reach it and get into difficulties.

SAFE TO SWIM IN

Dogs tend to drink the water they swim in, so make sure it is safe and watch out for any tell-tale signs of illness afterwards. Rinse the dog's skin and eyes after swimming to avoid any irritation from chemicals in the water.

67

Most dogs cope perfectly well with swimming. But if you are in doubt – for example if your dog is old or very unfit – check with the vet first.

AGILITY

Dog agility involves a type of obstacle course which tests the animal's fitness and owner's skill in training. It is fun for the dog and the owner, as well as being good exercise for both. You may first come across agility equipment at general puppy training classes – if you find it is something you and your dog enjoy, you can carry on doing it for fun, or even work up to competing at an international level. As well as the health benefits, it is also a good way to keep your dog obedient and happy, and to help you develop a closer relationship.

PRINCIPLES OF AGILITY

The time it takes to complete the obstacle course is timed, and you also drop marks for mistakes. No treats are allowed, and the handler must not touch the dog, so must use only his voice and gestures for control. This means that the dog must be very well trained to succeed. The dog depends on human direction to complete the course, which is fairly complicated and different each time.

THE OBSTACLES

Typical obstacles include: hurdles, rising spread jump, brush fence, hoop, table, long jump, water jump, tunnels, weaving poles and ramps.

THE COMPETITION

In a competition situation, the course is configured by the judge. The handler is given a map of the course beforehand to work out the strategy for completion. Often the handler will take a slightly different route around the course from the dog to avoid the obstacles, so this needs to be taken into account. Dog and handler only get one attempt at the course, so careful planning is vital.

68

Many dog training centres offer specialist training sessions in agility if you are interested in taking it further.

THE PENALTIES

Typical penalties include: time fault (taking too long to complete the course), missed contact, dropped bar, off-course, refusal or handler error, such as touching the dog or an obstacle. Other faults include the dog biting the judge, the handler taking toys and treats into the ring or the dog leaving the ring.

4 DIET

Achieving a feeding regime that works for your dog is crucial. The range of foods available can seem overwhelming, but once you find one that suits your dog, stick to it. Food is vital to your dog's physical health but can also have an effect on its behaviour. You will need to monitor the amount and frequency of feeding carefully to avoid making your dog obese. As well as the complete food you feed your dog every day, it is likely that you will also use treats to help in training it. These need to be considered as part of the overall calorie intake as they can quickly add up.

There can be problems associated with feeding – from sickness and diarrhoea to the dog eating grass and even faeces. Poisoning and bowel obstructions can happen all too easily, and you should be vigilant in preventing these as they can prove fatal.

TYPES OF DIET

Dogs need food for energy – for exercise and bodily functions – as well as for growth and keeping the body in top condition. Just as humans do, they need a balance of nutrients, including proteins, fats, vitamins, minerals and water. Carbohydrates are not essential for dogs, but they can use them as a source of energy. There are different types of dog food available – tinned, semi-moist and dry – and most are "complete", so in theory, they should meet all your dog's dietary needs.

CHOOSING A TYPE

"Complete" dry foods are often based on chicken and rice or corn. The better quality food you buy, the less your dog will need. You can moisten the food with a little warm water to begin with to make it easier for your dog to eat. Semi-moist and tinned foods also vary in quality – choose the best you can afford. Again, most formulations are "complete" and should not need to be supplemented. The choice you make depends on personal preference and what suits your dog best.

MIXING FOOD

If you choose to, you can mix a little moist tinned food with a dry diet to make it more interesting for your dog, though there is generally no need to do this. Or you can add "mixer" to tinned food to vary the texture.

Once you have found a diet that suits your dog, avoid changing it. Food that works with your dog's digestion will result in dark brown, formed faeces.

70

Treats are fine, but remember that chocolate is poisonous to dogs – it takes a lot of time and effort for their livers to process it – and in some cases, can even be fatal. Dark chocolate is especially dangerous, and small dogs are most at risk. Always choose treats that are specially formulated for dogs and don't overuse them.

71

Raw or lightly cooked vegetables are a good source of vitamins and minerals and are perfectly safe to give to dogs. You can use them as treats, for example. Avoid potatoes, though, as these cause diarrhoea and flatulence.

72

Different dogs have different dietary needs. Dogs that work hard will have a high energy requirement and can be given a concentrated diet. Other dogs may need a "light" diet as they need fewer calories. There are even special diets for dogs with clinical conditions such as kidney disease.

FREQUENCY AND QUANTITY OF FEEDING

It's important to get the frequency and quantity of feeding right to keep your dog in optimum health. Most adult dogs need only one or two meals a day. You need to provide your dog with enough energy for its lifestyle, as well as materials for its body to be able to grow and regenerate. You must avoid giving too much food though, which will result in your dog becoming obese (see page 70).

SUPPLEMENTS

"Complete" dog foods should contain all the nutrients your dog needs. You may choose to supplement your dog's diet with vitamins and minerals, but consult your vet before you do and read the label carefully. Oversupplementation can be as dangerous as deficiency can.

73

The following factors mean that you may need to feed your dog more than usual for its size: an especially active lifestyle, living out of doors, pregnancy and lactation or growing quickly (in the case of puppies).

FEEDING TIME

Don't allow your dog to eat the same food as you at the same time. It should have its own separate bowl, and it should eat after you do. Not only is your food likely to be unsuitable for your dog, leading to possible obesity and digestive problems, but allowing it to share your mealtimes will upset the hierarchical order of eating, and your dog may develop dominance-related behaviour problems (see page 40).

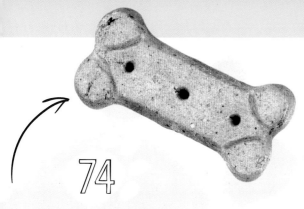

74

If you feed your dog treats, remember that these should account for no more than 15 per cent of the total daily food intake. You will have to reduce the amount of other food you give to balance this.

75

Don't leave uneaten food in your dog's bowl. Remove any leftovers after 20 minutes. If your dog does not eat all of its food, you may be giving it too much.

PUPPIES' DIETS

Puppies have specific needs when it comes to food. They need plenty of energy for activity, as well as materials for growth and development. Specially formulated puppy foods are rich in calories, protein, vitamins and minerals; there should be no need for any supplements. A puppy will need two or three times as much food as an adult dog in relation to its body size.

FEEDING AND SICKNESS

The feeding habits of your dog are closely linked to its general well-being; they may be the cause or a symptom of a problem. Food also has an important role to play in nursing your dog back to heath if it has been ill. Dogs will try to eat almost anything and will often scavenge. You need to keep your dog from eating anything that could cause a bowel obstruction or be poisonous.

VOMITING AND DIARRHOEA

Vomiting and diarrhoea can be caused by changes in diet, scavenging, stress, drinking milk or drinking too much water. Try to keep your dog from scavenging for food when out walking. If your dog is vomiting frequently and is lethargic, take it to the vet. If it is eager to eat, try feeding it a small amount after twelve hours and gradually build up to normal meals. Only allow small amounts of water at first to keep it from vomiting again and becoming dehydrated.

POISONING

Poisoning is serious and potentially fatal. Your dog is at risk of poisoning from various household and garden chemicals, including detergents, disinfectants, weed and insect killers and paints. Human medicines are also dangerous; while it is possible that some could be used to treat dogs, the doses would probably be different. Signs of poisoning include vomiting, weakness, convulsions and collapse. If you suspect poisoning, take the dog to the vet with as much information as you can gather about the cause.

EATING GRASS

You may see your dog eating grass; this is usually nothing to worry about, as long as the grass is not treated with chemicals. The dog will usually vomit the grass back up or simply pass it out in the faeces. Dogs often eat grass if their digestive systems feel uncomfortable to induce vomiting. Consult the vet if the problem persists, the dog has no appetite and is losing weight.

76

When your dog is convalescing, try cooking it small meals of fresh meat such as chicken or fish (rather than red meat). Serve the food warm; hand-feeding will make it especially appealing.

77

Bowel obstruction is a common problem. A dog's digestive system can become blocked by many things: children's toys, stones, balls or bones, for example. Avoid giving your dog bones – they can also splinter and damage the mouth, stomach and intestines. Any kind of bowel obstruction can result in major surgery, so try to avoid it.

78

Cat and dog food may look similar, but you shouldn't feed cat food to your dog – it is much richer in protein. The dog's body will break down the surplus protein into waste products but, over time, this will put a strain on the kidneys.

OBESITY

Obesity can be a problem for dogs, just as it is for humans. It affects up to half of all dogs in developed countries, but it is avoidable – in fact, it is usually caused by owners overfeeding their dogs. As well as causing serious health problems, obesity will also affect a dog's quality of life. It may not feel like running around or playing, and in summer, it will overheat due to the insulating effect of its layer of fat.

EFFECTS OF NEGLECT

Many dog owners lead busy lives. It can be difficult to find time to exercise your dog every day or to think about its diet. But the effects of neglecting these things can be serious and life-threatening. Obese dogs are susceptible to heart failure, diabetes, bronchitis and arthritis. They are likely to suffer problems with their skin, eyes and paws. If they need an operation, they are also more at risk under the anaesthetic if they are overweight.

79

It's easy to fall into the trap of treating your dog – especially if it is adept at begging for food. But even small treats given regularly can add up to a significant amount of extra calories over time, causing your dog to put on weight gradually. You may not even notice until your dog is badly overweight.

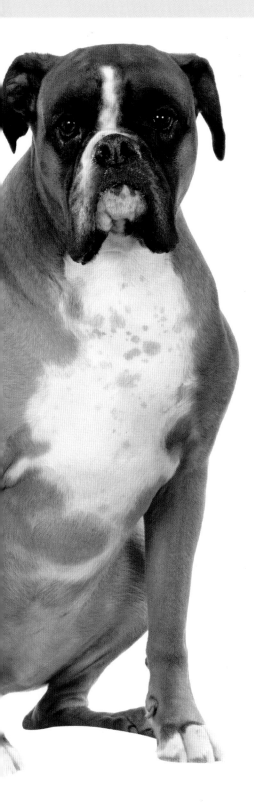

To tell if your dog is obese, run your hands along the sides of its body from head to tail. If your dog has a weight problem, you will be able to feel the fat on its sides, around the neck and at the base of the tail.

LOSING WEIGHT

To lose weight, your dog needs to eat less food and exercise more. A simple way to achieve this is to reduce the amount of food you give it at mealtimes and to cut out treats entirely (aside from "healthy" treats such as fruit and vegetables). Never put a dog on a crash diet; instead, reduce its food intake gradually. If you increase the amount of exercise you are giving your dog, again, increase this gradually. Remember that a severly overweight dog may be reluctant to exercise.

FOOD AND BEHAVIOUR

Food has a strong link to your dog's behaviour. At a chemical level, proper, balanced nutrition should mean that you have a calm, happy dog. A poor-quality, erratic diet can likewise result in a bad-tempered and hard-to-control pet. On a psychological level, the way you feed your dog and the times at which you offer it food can have a profound effect on its behaviour and its relationship with you and your family.

EATING FAECES

Dogs like to eat almost anything – including, sometimes, their own or other animals' faeces (this is known as coprophagia). If you give your dog plenty of stimulation to keep it from becoming bored, it will probably grow out of the problem.

Most dogs are food-oriented, so treats make great incentives during training (see pages 74 to 89). Remember to count any treats you give as part of the dog's daily calorie intake.

HYPERACTIVITY

Too much cereal in your dog's food in the form of wheat or corn can cause it to become hyperactive, unfocused and difficult to train. If you suspect this is a problem, test a food for high levels of cereal by soaking it in water for 15 minutes. If it swells up and goes mushy, it is high in cereal content. If you subsequently make changes to the dog's diet, remember to do this gradually.

FOOD AND DOMINANCE

In the wild, dogs hunt their food in packs. Once they have made the kill, the pack eats – starting with the leaders. In your home, you should establish you and your family as the pack leaders (see page 40); this means that you always eat first. If you let your dog eat at the same time as you, this will upset the order, and it may cause the dog to develop dominance-related behaviour problems. Likewise, if the dog begs and is given scraps from the table, it will remember its success and begin to feel dominant.

5 INTRODUCTION TO TRAINING

Training your dog is desirable for a number of reasons. If your dog can respond to at least a few very basic commands – for instance, if you can tell it to stay and trust it to do so – this will keep the dog safe when you are out and about, and may even save its life. Such basic commands will also make the dog more acceptable in social situations. A certain degree of training is therefore part of your responsibility as a dog owner.

More than this, though, training can be a rewarding experience for you and your dog. Above all, your dog wants to please you and to know its place in the hierarchy of the "pack". Training can be great fun for both of you.

There are various methods of training. You may choose to go it alone, or you might decide to join a training class, which can provide a supportive and helpful environment that is as much about educating you as your dog. Nowadays, it is generally accepted that the best way to get results is to use positive reinforcement methods, which involve rewarding good behaviour rather than punishing bad – kinder to your dog and also much more effective.

TRAINING BASICS

Training your dog is essential not only for its well-being – a trained dog is a happy dog – but also so that it behaves in a way that is acceptable to you and the other people the dog will encounter. Theories about training dogs have changed over the years, but the currently accepted best practice is based on a system of positive reinforcement, which means that you praise and reward your dog when it does what you want it to.

PRINCIPLES OF POSITIVE REINFORCEMENT

If the dog behaves well, and responds to a command, then give it a positive response. If it comes to associate good behaviour with a positive outcome it is very likely to repeat the behaviour. Conversely, if good behaviour goes ignored, then it is likely that the dog will simply stop that pattern of behaviour and not repeat it.

82

The order of training is as follows: give the command; praise your dog when he does what you want; give him a treat.

CONSISTENCY

The most important thing to remember when you are training your dog is to be consistent. Essentially, the dog needs to know its name, as this is what you should say to get its attention before giving a command. Always use the same command for a particular kind of behaviour. You must avoid confusing your dog at all costs.

83

Reward your dog effectively with food or lavish praise – both verbal and physical. The food you give can be healthy titbits such as vegetables, or treats built into the daily calorie intake.

84

Never hit your dog to discipline it. This is not only illegal in many parts of the world, but is unlikely to have the desired effect.

85

Train your dog little and often to avoid boredom on both sides!

POSITIVE REINFORCEMENT

In the past, dog training involved punishing the dog for bad or undesirable behaviour. Now, it is understood that a far better (and more pleasant) way to train a dog is by rewarding and praising good and desirable behaviour.

A LITTLE PSYCHOLOGY

Your dog knows its place in the "pack" (see pages 40–1) and wants nothing more than to please you. If it comes to associate patterns of behaviour with positive outcomes – it can see that you are pleased, and is rewarded for pleasing you – it will repeat them. Once a pattern of behaviour is learned, it is no longer necessary to reward the dog for responding to commands (though praise is always good). Similarly, if you simply ignore any bad or undesirable behaviour, your lack of response should mean that the dog will stop doing it.

REWARDS

Rewards for positive behaviour can take the form of snacks – food is always good for getting results. Try small pieces of carrot, cheese, cooked liver or sausage. Alternatively, offering a favourite toy might be an option. Some dogs will respond well simply to lavish praise and attention from you. You can also use a combination of these methods – find out what works best for you and your dog. If food is to be the reward, make it something small and very tasty. If it takes your dog too long to eat it, it may forget what it was being rewarded for.

86

If you reward your dog with food, remember to count any titbits you give as part of its daily calorie intake.

DETERRENTS

You should never punish a dog for bad behaviour. However, there are two kinds of deterrent that you can try. First, simply ignore bad behaviour. If this doesn't work, send the dog out of the room until it stops whatever it was doing. A different approach is to create a diversion. Try making a sudden noise, by throwing something onto the ground. Or squirt the dog with water to surprise it (aim at the body, not the head). When the dog stops its bad behaviour, give it a reward as usual.

87

Whichever reward method you find
motivates your dog, remember that
you will need to be able to offer
it whenever your dog does
something good.

88

Your dog has a very short
memory span – around half a
second – so it is vital to reward
any good behaviour straight
away in order for the dog to
make a connection between
the two.

HOUSE-TRAINING

Until they are about three weeks old, puppies are stimulated to relieve themselves by their mother's licking them. At around that age a newborn puppy begins instinctively to leave its nest in order to urinate and defecate.

At around eight weeks old, they start to move farther from the nest and use habitual locations for this purpose. This is when house-training – the art of encouraging a puppy to use grass rather than carpet as its toilet – can begin.

GIVE HIM TIME

House-training problems often arise when you think the puppy has urinated or defecated but in fact it hasn't. You need to be aware that puppies often need about 15 minutes of sniffing around the garden before they are ready to relieve themselves. Never rush the puppy through its time outdoors in less than 20 minutes.

USING POSITIVE REINFORCEMENT

Always show your pleasure and reward the dog for performing outside. Conversely, you must never punish the dog for urinating or defecating indoors. Shouting at your puppy will only make it anxious to avoid your displeasure, and may lead it to eat its own faeces to avoid your anger.

89

Puppies need to urinate more frequently than adult dogs – approximately once an hour – so be prepared to take it to the garden often. A puppy will always need to relieve itself when it wakes up, about 20 minutes after eating, after play and when it gets excitable (for example, after meeting a visitor).

Good
Dog

90

The first place to take a puppy new to your home is the garden. Walk it around until he has relieved itself, and praise it for this. Immediately the puppy will start to understand where you want it to go to the toilet.

PROBLEM DOGS

If your puppy urinates or defecates in your home, you need to use an enzyme-based cleaner (sold by pet stores and vets) to really break down the scent. If this is not done correctly, the dog will be able to detect the scent and will begin to learn to use that space as a toilet area. If the puppy often wakes up in the night and soils its bedding, be sure the temperature is sufficiently warm: getting cold at night will make the dog need to relieve itself.

STARTING TRAINING

You might ask, why bother to train your dog? Dogs instinctively want to help humans and "work" for them – not just the "working" breeds, but others too. Training reinforces the bond between you, and makes the dog feel more secure and purposeful. It's important to do it right, though, to set yourself up for years of problem-free good behaviour. You may decide to get professional help in the form of dog training classes – which are targeted as much at you, the owner, as your dog!

TRAINING CLASSES

Dog-training classes are a great way of making sure you have covered the basics and are fulfilling your responsibilities as a dog owner. They should give you a thorough grounding in good training habits that you can continue in your spare time.

CHOOSING A CLASS

Before committing yourself to a particular class, go and have a look around. Go along armed with questions to ask yourself and any other owners you meet. Are the trainers friendly and helpful? Do they enjoy what they do? Is everyone in the class included and encouraged? Does the environment seem well controlled? And do the dogs being trained seem happy and well behaved?

91

Bad training habits:
• Hitting your dog –
absolutely forbidden
• Telling the dog off
• Confusing language, signals
and gestures
• Inconsistent techniques
• Long, boring training
sessions

92

Good training habits:
• Positive reinforcement
• Plenty of attention and praise
• Training in short, sharp bursts
• Clear command words
• Clicker training, used correctly

TRAINING PROBLEMS

Training can be a long and sometimes frustrating process. But often the problems that arise have simple explanations and can be easily solved.

GETTING YOUR DOG'S ATTENTION

One of the most basic training problems is not being able to get your dog's attention. The right way to get your dog's attention is by using its name. Your dog should turn and look at you when you say its name – and if it doesn't, you need to teach it to do so. Hold a treat in your hand, out to one side. Call your dog's name. It should turn towards you but will probably look at the treat and not at you. Keep saying its name until it looks directly at you, and, as soon as that happens, reward it with the treat.

INCONSISTENT COMMANDS

Simple confusion is one of the most basic training problems for your dog. It is crucial that you use the same command word or phrase every time for a particular action. Even if you are sure you always use the same words, make sure that everyone else involved in training the dog or giving commands uses the same words too.

LOSS OF CONCENTRATION

Training can be an intensive process and it is likely that you and your dog will become bored or tired over the course of a training session. To avoid this, train in short bursts – little and often is best. If you feel at any time that you or your dog are losing concentration, it's time to stop. Training should be a fun experience for both of you – not a chore.

93

Don't attempt to train your dog when it has just eaten. As so many training techniques rely on food as a reward, withhold the meal immediately before a training session.

CORE COMMANDS

Even if you don't intend to win any prizes for dog obedience training, there are some basic, "core" commands you should teach your dog. At the very least you should expect your dog to respond to "stay" and "down". This is for its own safety as well as to make it socially acceptable. "Stay", in particular, is a command that could save your dog's life.

SIT

Teach your dog to sit by standing in front of it with a treat. As it is looking up at you, move the treat backwards above its head. The dog will have to start to sit to keep following the treat with its eyes. As the dog's knees bend, say "sit". As the dog's bottom makes contact with the floor, reward it with the treat and praise it lavishly. Keep repeating this exercise, gradually replacing the treat with praise alone.

STAY

Two good examples of when you might want your dog to stay are if someone comes to your house and knocks at the door (you don't want your dog to rush and greet them), or if you are out and about and your dog wants to investigate something it shouldn't. In both these situations it is vital that you trust your dog to respond to your command. Teach your dog to stay by first getting it to sit. Once it is sitting, slowly back away from the dog, holding out the flat of your hand. As you move away, and the dog remains still, say "stay". Praise the dog for staying still. Repeat this technique, gradually moving further away each time.

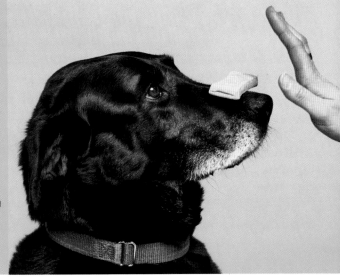

DOWN

Teach your dog to lie down using the following method. Sit down beside your dog, with a tasty treat in your hand. Show the dog the treat, under one of your outstretched legs. The dog will try to reach the treat and to do this will have to lie right down with its tummy on the ground. As the dog assumes this position, and only then, say the command word – "down" – and give him the treat. Down is an important command, but it may take a while for you both to master it, so be patient.

94

Whenever you see your dog lie down around the house, say "down" and praise and reward him straight away. He will soon come to associate the command with the action.

CLICKER TRAINING

Clicker training involves the use of a small, handheld device to make a clicking sound at the moment when the dog does something you want him to – and at the same time, you reward him. The clicker gives a more consistent sound than voiced praise (it is not dependent on your tone of voice or mood), and is more instant. The dog learns to associate the click with good behaviour and the ensuing reward.

STEPS TO CLICKER TRAINING

Clicker training works by tapping into the dog's long-term memory. It can be a very effective method of training, but only if you do it right. There are many books and resources on the internet devoted to the subject of clicker training, which is relatively new and quite revolutionary. For it to work it is vital to follow the steps precisely.

1. First, teach your dog that when you click, it gets a treat. Click, then drop a treat for it, repeatedly. Do this again and again, until it knows that a click will quickly be followed by something it wants.

2. Next, whenever your dog does what you want it to do – without you telling it to do it – click and drop a reward.

3. Finally, introduce the command word into the sequence. When your dog does what you want it to do, say the command word, click and drop a reward.

95

For clicker training to work, the dog must only ever associate the sound of the clicker with a positive outcome.

96

When you click and give a reward, the idea is that the dog does not associate these occurrences with you. Remain calm and try to dissociate yourself from the actions.

97

As with any other training technique, it is important that you only reward desirable behaviour.

HAPPY TRAINING

The important thing about clicker training is the dog discovers for itself by trial and error what good behaviour is. It will enjoy figuring out how to please you and get a reward. You should see that once the dog is trained, it seems to really love responding to your commands.

6 PLAYTIME

Bonding with your dog isn't only about teaching it who's boss. Sometimes it's good for you and your pet to have some fun. But successful play can also be constructive and educational, as well as a great source of exercise for both of you. Experiment and see what is most enjoyable for your dog.

PLAY BASICS

Playing with your dog is a great way of giving it extra exercise, mental stimulation and attention; it's also a good way of bonding with your dog and can work as an extension of training. Play should always happen when you initiate it (not your dog). It is important to establish some ground rules as a framework for constructive play.

LEARNING TO PLAY

In the wild, dogs learn vital hunting and defence skills through playing with their mother and littermates. So, puppies that have no playmates between six weeks and six months old (most domestic puppies kept as pets) miss out on learning how to play and will need to be taught. Playing is a type of behaviour that your dog can learn just like any other.

APPROPRIATE GAMES

The types of games your dog will readily play may depend in part on its breed. For example, retrievers will, fairly obviously, enjoy playing "fetch" type games in which you throw an object and the dog brings it back to you. Other dogs may not get as much out of this kind of game. Terriers will enjoy shaking and "killing" an object, as their ancestors would naturally have done with prey.

PROPS AND TOYS

An example of a very useful toy that you can buy is a "kong" – a hollow, ridged rubber cone that has a hole at either end. The holes are too small for the dog to get its nose inside, and the kong will bounce irregularly. This makes it ideal for throwing games, or for filling with tidbits of food. Trying to extract the food can keep a dog happily occupied for a long time! Other good toys for dogs include balls (big enough not to be swallowed), or even old towels or slippers.

98

Don't let your dog get the upper hand, even in play. You should always initiate play, and if there is a "winner" in the game, it should be you.

GREAT IDEAS FOR GAMES

Here are some ideas for games that you and your dog will enjoy. Once you've mastered the basic techniques, you can adapt them to incorporate whatever toys or props you have to hand.

FETCH

Many dogs love fetching objects, and the wonderful thing about this simple game is that if you do it right, your dog gets plenty of exercise and you can stand still for much of the time! Start off by getting your dog interested in the toy or object you are holding by wiggling it around, then toss it a short distance away and say "fetch". As soon as your dog picks the object up, attract its attention by clapping and moving away, encouraging it to come to you. When it does, say "drop it" and reward it when it drops the object at your feet. Immediately throw the object again and say "fetch" so that it understands that the game will continue. You can gradually increase the distance that you throw the object.

CATCH

Start off by trying to get your dog to catch small pieces of food, before moving onto larger objects. Learning to catch is a good way for your dog to develop its co-ordination, as well as being excellent exercise for stamina and flexibility. You can even buy special dog frisbees; avoid using an ordinary frisbee, as it can damage a dog's teeth and mouth.

99

As with training your dog, don't play for too long at any one time. Short, sharp bursts of structured play are best.

HIDE-AND-SEEK

Take a treat and go and hide in another room. Call your dog into the room and wait for it to find you. When it does, reward it with the treat. Start off by hiding somewhere very simple. You can gradually build up the difficulty of the game as your dog comes to understand that when it finds you, it will be rewarded!

7 INTRODUCTION TO GROOMING

Grooming is important to maintain a good standard of hygiene, prevent infections and to give your dog a general sense of health and well-being. Establish a daily and weekly grooming routine at an early age – if your puppy is accustomed to being brushed and washed as well as having its ears and eyes examined and cleaned, it is less likely to object to this treatment later in life.

Essential grooming care includes brushing your dog's teeth, washing its eyes and ears regularly, brushing its coat and clipping its nails. Every so often, you will want (or need!) to give your dog a bath as well.

BRUSHING AND NAILCARE

Regular grooming promotes a healthy coat by physically removing dead hairs and skin cells, and stimulating the blood supply to the skin. Your dog will feel invigorated after a thorough brushing. A well-groomed dog is happier too because you will feel more affectionate towards it when it is clean and fresh-smelling. Every so often you will need to have your dog's nails clipped.

A HEALTHY COAT

Of course, dogs' coats vary enormously. Some dogs have very short, dense hair, while others have thin, wispy coats. Many are long-haired breeds with coats that need a great deal of attention. Wire-haired breeds have a coarse outer coat with a soft underlayer that will need to be regularly thinned out. In general, though, all healthy coats look glossy and shiny, and the skin you can see underneath will be clean pink or black with no flakes.

100

There are several types of brushes available; choose the most suitable kind for your dog's coat. For short-haired breeds such as labradors, use a rubber brush. For long- or bristle-haired dogs such as collies, choose a wire-pin brush. For dogs that have thin hair, go carefully and gently with a softer, bristle-haired brush to avoid scratching the skin.

NAIL CLIPPING

Your dog's nails will need to be clipped regularly. Check the dog's feet every week to make sure they are in good condition in general. The nails should just touch the ground when the dog is standing. If the nails do need clipping, you can do this yourself, or get a professional groomer or the vet to do it for you. Nail clipping must be done carefully to avoid cutting the "quick", which will bleed and be painful for your dog.

HOW TO BRUSH

Brush your dog starting at its back end and work towards the front. Stroke upwards around the sides and chest to aerate the coat. Finish off by brushing the coat back down in the direction of growth.

101

Most dogs love being brushed. It's a time when they know they have your full attention!

102

Take special care not to brush too hard as you work around the tail area. It can be very sensitive in some breeds.

EAR AND EYE CARE

You should keep your dog's ears and eyes clean, and the best time to do this is as part of the weekly grooming session. Ears in particular are susceptible to collecting dirt and debris, and even becoming infected. You should also watch out for foreign bodies that may get into your pet's eyes or ears when you are out and about, such as parasites or plant seeds.

EAR ANATOMY

Dogs' ears are prone to collecting moisture and wax due to their shape. The outside part of the ear is the "ear flap" which may be small and pricked up, or long and floppy. From here, the ear canal runs close to the side of the head, then slopes inwards towards the eardrum. The eardrum is a thin membrane that can be easily ruptured. The ear canal is easily infected, especially in dogs with long ear flaps and lots of hair in their ears. Try to keep the ears relatively hair-free, if possible.

CLEANING THE EARS

Choose an ear wash formulated for dogs. Soak some absorbent cotton on the ear wash and squeeze out the excess. Gently wipe inside the ears, rubbing up and down. Next, soak a cotton swab in the ear wash and gently clean the hard-to-reach places. (Don't push the cotton swab too far in or force it in any way.) After you have finished cleaning, encourage your dog to shake its head to get rid of the excess moisture.

When cleaning your dog's ears, don't poke around right inside the ear canal. Leave this to the vet.

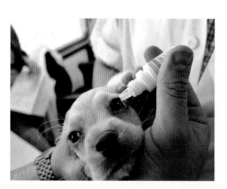

CLEANING THE EYES

Clean your dog's eyes using a piece of cotton wool and special eyewash, or plain water. Gently wipe around the eye area, cleaning away any discharge that has collected at the corners. Be careful not to poke the eye itself.

104

Warm any ear wash you will be using up to room temperature before applying it, to make the ear-cleaning process as comfortable as possible for your dog.

105

Healthy eyes are bright and clear, with no cloudiness, redness or discharge.

DENTAL CARE

In the wild, dogs eat all parts of animals, including the bones, which helps to keep their teeth clean. It's not safe to feed your dog bones, as they splinter, so you need to help your pet keep its teeth clean as part of a daily hygiene routine. Bad breath in dogs is common, but it's not normal or natural, and is a sign of poor dental hygiene – which must be treated.

PLAQUE

Just as it does in humans, the enamel of dogs' teeth collects a coating of plaque, formed by food debris, saliva and bacteria. This starts to build up as soon as the dog's adult teeth come through. If you don't remove the plaque, it forms a hard layer called calculus. This can spread beneath the gumline and inflame the gums. Eventually this will lead to gum disease and may cause the teeth to fall out.

106

There are different types of dog toothbrushes available, including double-headed electric ones and manual versions that fit over the end of your finger.

107

Dry food and chews can help keep your dog's teeth clean, in conjunction with regular brushing.

BRUSHING TEETH

You should get into the habit of brushing your dog's teeth every day. Lift the lip until you can see the teeth. Gently rub some specially formulated dog toothpaste onto the teeth with your finger. Brush gently, using a small, soft toothbrush. Concentrate especially on the outsides of the teeth and the back molars, which can accumulate a lot of debris. Don't brush too vigorously or attack the gums.

108

Before brushing, get your dog used to having its mouth handled. Gently lift the lip, saying "teeth" as you do so. Once the dog has let you access the teeth, praise him for letting you do this.

BATHING

You shouldn't need to bathe your dog very often, unless it is exceptionally dirty, but an occasional bath is a great way to keep it feeling in top condition. It is a myth that all dogs hate baths. If you introduce a bathing routine from when the dog is a puppy, there should be no problem. Praise and reward the dog for good behaviour during bathtime, just as you would at any other time.

DOGS LOVE DIRT

Dogs love strong smells and seem drawn to what we think of as "dirt". You may find that when you go for a walk, your dog will want to swim in filthy water, dig around in sticky mud and even roll in other dogs' faeces. Rolling in faeces is quite normal behaviour; their smells tells your dog a lot about the animal that deposited them. But if you can't stop it from doing this, it will definitely mean that you will want to give your pet a bath as soon as possible!

BATH PRACTICALITIES

Giving your dog a bath every couple of months should be sufficient. If you bathe it any more often then than that, use a specially formulated dog shampoo and conditioner to avoid washing away all of the natural oils from the hair and skin. You could also use a mild baby shampoo.

BATH TECHNIQUE

Fill a plastic tub with lukewarm water, sit the dog in it and wet it all over, using a cup to scoop up water. Wet its face using your hands. Lather shampoo all over the body, leave it for a minute, and then rinse it off thoroughly. Repeat with the conditioner, if you are using it. Once your dog is clean, wrap it in a warm, dry towel, and rub vigorously. Always dry your dog thoroughly to keep it from getting chilled. On a hot day, it can finish drying outside in the garden, or you can finish it off yourself with a hairdryer.

109

Groom your dog thoroughly before bathing it to remove any tangles from the hair.

8 HEALTHCARE

Over the course of its life, it is almost inevitable that your dog will suffer some form of illness or health problem. Many conditions will be minor, temporary or easily treatable. However, it is important to know when a symptom indicates a potentially serious or life-threatening condition, so you can act quickly and seek professional help.

This chapter gives a broad overview of some of the most common medical problems, as well as preventative treatments. But the most important thing, if in doubt about your dog's health, is to seek advice from a vet. Get to know your dog and understand the signs that indicate that it is in good general health, and the signs that indicate that it is distressed or in pain.

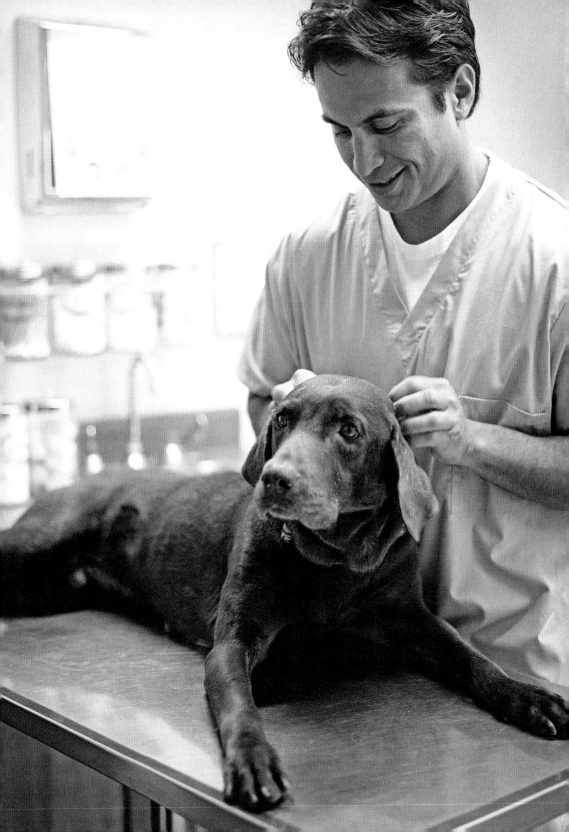

GENERAL HEALTH

You probably know when your dog is in good general health. A healthy dog is responsive and alert. It has a glossy coat and holds and moves itself easily. It probably also has a cool, wet nose. By contrast, a dog that is unwell will seem listless and have a dull, dry coat. It may hunch its body and hang its tail between its legs. Beyond these general indicators, there are also other signs you can check for to assess the well-being of your dog.

EATING AND DRINKING

It may seem obvious, but a healthy dog will have an appetite for food and drink. Drinking and eating less than usual is a cause for concern – as is drinking far more or more frequently. Likewise, look out for any changes in defecation or urination. Most dogs defecate around two or three times a day, and the faeces should be firm, with no signs of blood or mucus. Frequency of urination varies enormously from dog to dog. The most important thing is to become familiar with your dog's own habits and be sensitive to any change.

The usual place to take your dog's temperature is in its rectum. Lubricate the thermometer with petroleum jelly before inserting it.

TEMPERATURE

A healthy dog's nose is likely to be moist (though this is not always the case). There are many mucus glands and fluid ducts around the nose area, and part of the reason for this is temperature regulation. Moisture evaporating from the nose lowers the dog's temperature. An overheated dog or one that has a fever will probably have a warm, dry nose. The normal temperature range for a dog is 37.7–38.9°C (100–102°F). A high temperature is known as pyrexia, and is probably due to an infection.

111

You can find a pulse point on your dog's inner thigh (a vet can show you exactly where). Take the pulse for 30 seconds and double the number to find the beats per minute.

PULSE AND RESPIRATION

A normal pulse rate for a dog can be anywhere between 70 and 160 beats per minute. It depends on the size, age and fitness of the dog. Excitement, fear, overheating and shock (low blood pressure) can all cause the pulse rate to rise. A normal respiratory rate is between 10 and 30 breaths per minute when the dog is resting. A dog that is having trouble breathing will appear to find it an effort and may be using its abdominal muscles.

112

Again, count respirations for 30 seconds and double the number for breaths per minute. Only take respiration and pulse rates when the dog is resting.

PARASITES

There are two main types of parasites – ectoparasites (which live outside the body) and endoparasites (which live inside the body). Examples of ectoparasites that affect dogs are fleas and ticks. Endoparasites include a variety of worms, which may live in the digestive tract, or even in the lungs, blood cells, heart, muscle, liver or brain of the dog. Endoparasites can be dangerous to the dog's health and even life-threatening, while ectoparasites are generally merely irritating. All should be treated.

FLEAS

It should be obvious if your dog has fleas. It will scratch itself, bite its coat and appear uncomfortable. You may see fleas (which are small and black) on its coat, or on carpets or furniture. Once you have established that your dog has fleas, you should treat it to remove them. Treatments target either the adult fleas or the eggs. The most effective are now considered to be "spot-on" treatments, a few drops of which are applied to the scruff of the neck. Treatments also come in the form of powders or sprays, or may be given orally.

TICKS AND MITES

Ticks are small arachnids that live on the skin of infected dogs. They feed on blood, eventually swelling up to the size of a pea. You are most likely to find them on the dog's head or abdomen, where the hair cover is not very dense. When the tick is removed, it is essential that the mouthparts are removed completely, or they could cause infection. It is best to ask a vet to remove any ticks you find. Mange mites are tiny arachnids that live in the hair follicles or just beneath the surface of the skin. They are treated with special shampoo or mange wash; consult your vet

WORMS

Dogs can get roundworms, tapeworms, hookworms, whipworms and heartworms. They pick up worms easily when they are out and about, sniffing where other dogs have been (especially the faeces). Worm eggs and larvae that get onto the dog's coat are then swallowed when the dog grooms itself. A dog with worms may have no symptoms, or it may have vomiting, diarrhoea, weight loss or a pot-bellied look. You should worm your dog regularly – ask the vet to recommend a suitable treatment.

113

If you have more than one dog, but only one seems affected by parasites, you should still treat them all.

114

Dogs excrete worm eggs in their faeces, which is one reason why you must clean up after your dog. Some worms can infect humans. Always wash your hands after cleaning up after your dog.

115

A pregnant bitch should be wormed – some types of muscle-dwelling worms activate during pregnancy and can pass across the placenta to the unborn puppies.

HOT DOGS

Dogs do not have a very efficient system for cooling down. This means that they are vulnerable to overheating and even heatstroke, which can be fatal.

PANTING

The main way a dog can lose heat to cool itself down is by panting. Panting is rapid breathing, during which the dog opens its mouth and lets the tongue hang out. The surfaces of the inside of the mouth and the tongue are wet, and as air passes over them, it causes moisture to evaporate, which has a cooling action.

SWEATING

Dogs have sweat glands in various places but the only ones that cause visible sweat are on the pads of the feet (the others are all obscured by hair). So you may notice the pads of the feet sweating, but this does not contribute much to the dog's overall heat loss.

116

Because heat loss involves loss of moisture, it is essential that you give your dog plenty to drink when it is hot.

HEATSTROKE

If you suspect that your dog has heatstroke, you must act quickly or it could die. Symptoms include rapid panting, salivation and bright red lips and tongue. The dog may also show general signs of distress or even collapse. Move the dog to a cool place and cover it with wet towels or give it a cold shower. You could place it in a cold bath, but don't do this for more than a few minutes at a time. If the dog's condition does not improve, consult a vet immediately.

117

Never leave your dog in a closed room or a car on a hot day, and don't tie it up without access to shade and drinking water.

PREVENTATIVE TREATMENTS

All dogs need regular vaccinations to prevent disease. As well as preventing disease, you may choose to prevent your dog from becoming pregnant or siring puppies. One way to do this is to have your dog neutered or spayed – an operation that is usually performed (on either sex) when the dog is quite young.

VACCINATION

When a dog catches a disease, its immune system produces antibodies that make the dog resistant to catching the disease again. However, this is only useful if the dog survives the initial attack, and sadly, many don't. Vaccines work by stimulating the immune system to produce antibodies against particular diseases, without the health risks of actually catching the disease. Ask your vet how often you should vaccinate your dog.

INTERNAL PARASITES

Many internal parasites are intestinal, such as hookworms, roundworms, whipworms and tapeworms. Steps towards prevention include examining your dog's faeces regularly, giving it deworming drugs (which may be combined with preventative treatment against heartworm), and keeping your pet from eating other dogs' faeces.

SPAYING

Spaying is a major abdominal operation and does carry some risks, such as haemorrage during recovery, and pain. The bitch will be sore for several days after the operation, though she can be given analgesic pain relief. The main reason for spaying a bitch is, of course, to prevent pregnancy. However, it also means that she no longer goes into heat (which can cause moodiness in some bitches), and that she cannot suffer from pyometra (infection of the uterus), which is a serious and life-threatening condition that can affect older females.

118

Spayed bitches have a reduced energy requirement, so they need less food than before to avoid becoming obese.

NEUTERING DOGS

Neutering a dog is a relatively minor procedure, in which a small incision is made at the front of the scrotum, through which the testicles are removed. The scrotum remains, but shrinks over the following weeks. As well as prevention of pregnancy, neutering a dog has other benefits. It is likely to display less aggressive, dominant or oversexed behaviour and cannot get testicular tumours. It is also less likely to develop tumours around the anus or prostate problems.

HEAT AND FALSE PREGNANCY

Every six months (or, in some breeds, every year) a female dog will "go into heat". This is the time when she is attractive to and receptive towards male dogs, and is fertile and so can become pregnant – also known as her oestrus cycle. The entire cycle lasts for a few weeks. The hormones produced by the cycle may produce a false pregnancy, during which time the bitch feels and acts as if she is pregnant, even when she is not.

PREVENTING HEAT

Though it is technically possible to prevent a bitch from experiencing heats through the use of hormones, this is dangerous to the pet, and vets would instead recommend spaying. If your bitch comes into heat and has an unplanned mating, it is possible to administer hormones to prevent an unwanted pregnancy.

THE SIGNS OF BEING IN HEAT

The first sign is an enlarged and reddened vulva. Soon, there will be a thin, bloody discharge, which gradually turns straw-coloured. The female will start producing pheromones that attract dogs – maybe from miles around – and she will show signs of being receptive to male attention. She will ovulate and after this, progesterone (a female hormone) levels rise for a few more weeks. By this time the bitch will either be pregnant or in a state of false pregnancy. After that, the hormone levels gradually fall again.

FALSE PREGNANCY

Two months after a heat, a female dog may experience a false pregnancy. This is quite normal. Signs include making "nests", adopting surrogate "puppies" in the form of soft toys and even producing milk. False pregnancy may cause the bitch to become nervous and her temperament may be affected. There is usually no need to treat a false pregnancy with hormones. Take away "adopted" objects and give your bitch plenty of exercise to help her through this time.

119

When a bitch is in heat, this is the only time when she will accept the advances of an amorous dog.

MATING, PREGNANCY AND WHELPING

You may decide that you want your bitch to have puppies. Although most bitches start to experience oestrus cycles from the age of around one, in some breeds it is not advisable for them to get pregnant until they are older. Check with your vet.

MATING

A bitch will only mate when she is in heat. During this time, allow her to mate with the chosen father 10 to 14 days from the start of her heat – a couple of times around 48 hours apart for the best chance of pregnancy. During mating, the dog mounts the bitch, inserts his penis into her vagina then thrusts for some time. After this, he may turn so the two are bottom to bottom but still joined. They may remain in this "tied" position for anywhere up to an hour – you shouldn't try to separate them.

PREGNANCY

Pregnancy in dogs can last anywhere between 54 and 72 days. It is difficult to be precise because the sperm can live for up to a week in the female's body before fertilization takes place. Around 30 days after mating, it should be possible for the vet to test for pregnancy. At first, there won't be outward signs, though the bitch may seem more affectionate. After five weeks, the mammary glands enlarge and redden, and after seven weeks she will start to "show" abdominal enlargement.

120

Feed a pregnant bitch a good, healthy diet, and increase the quantity slowly after the fifth week of pregnancy. She may prefer fewer, smaller meals to one large one.

WHELPING

The actual delivery of the puppies is known as "whelping". A few days before whelping, the bitch will probably seek out a place where she would like to give birth. Make sure that it's somewhere quiet and warm, with plenty of clean bedding to hand. A sign that the puppies are on the way in the next day is that the bitch's temperature drops and she starts producing milk. Most litters contain between four and eight pups, though anything between one and 12 is quite normal. When the puppies are born, the mother will break open the sac of membrane that surrounds them and chew through the umbilical cord (though you may have to help her with this).

121

Exercise a pregnant bitch as normal, but make the walks shorter once the pregnancy is very advanced.

122

Occasionally, a caesarean section is necessary to deliver a litter of puppies.

MISCELLANEOUS CONDITIONS

There are any number of relatively minor afflictions that may affect your dog. Some are more serious than others; most are treatable. Sometimes the reason for a particular symptom may not be clear, in which case consult a vet.

VOMITING

Dogs vomit for all kinds of reasons, but by far the most common cause is eating something inappropriate. This may simply be a food to which the dog has reacted badly, or it may be something more serious, such as a bone causing an intestinal obstruction. Observe your dog closely, and if the vomiting continues for more than 24 hours, consult your vet. Other causes of vomiting include poisoning, travel sickness and organ failure. With repeated vomiting, the dog is at risk of dehydration.

COUGHING

A common cause of coughing in dogs is tracheobronchitis, or "kennel cough", which is highly contagious. Vaccination only provides partial protection against this disease. Other causes of coughing include bronchitis, pneumonia, lung tumour, heartworm, lungworm and heart disease.

LAMENESS

Lameness means that a dog is not using one or more legs. It may stop using a leg totally or partially. Sometimes there is an obvious cause for the lameness, such as a trauma, strain, torn ligament or fracture. Or the dog may have stepped on a splinter or stone, or cut its foot. If you are not sure what is causing sudden (acute) lameness, check the affected limb carefully. Any severe lameness that doesn't improve with rest should be checked out by a vet.

HEARTWORMS

Canine heartworm disease is transmitted by mosquitoes, which pass the heartworm larvae into the dog's tissues when they bite it. The larvae migrate into the bloodstream and live in the heart and blood vessels. Male adult heartworms grow up to 15 cm (6 in) long and females up to 30 cm (12 in) long. There may be up to 250 living in one dog. If left untreated, they cause heart and lung disease and sometimes death. Treatment is possible, but prevention is better. Monthly tablets provide protection against heartworms and may also prevent infection by other internal parasites.

123

Your dog may have an itchy anus – you may notice it licking the area and dragging it along the ground – in which case it probably needs to have its anal sacs emptied. You will need to ask your vet to do this for you.

TIFFNESS

ny dogs develop
hritis, which causes
m to move stiffly. If this
ppens to your dog, you
n administer pain relief,
luding herbal remedies.
rt walks and swimming are
cellent parts of an exercise
ime for arthritic dogs.

ACCIDENTS AND EMERGENCIES

Your dog may suddenly become ill or in pain. You may or may not know the cause for this – but do try to assess any serious injuries before trying to treat them, and don't panic. Often you will need to get help from a vet. Whatever happens, remember that your dog will probably be frightened and may react to any attention aggressively. Try to remain calm.

ROAD ACCIDENT

If your dog is hit by a car, avoid moving it until you have assessed its injuries. (Move it to safety if it is in the middle of the road, though.) The most important thing is to ensure that the airway remains clear – it may become blocked by the dog's tongue if it is unconscious, or by vomit. Clear it with your finger if necessary. Look for broken bones and bleeding and move the dog as little as possible, though you must get it to a vet immediately. Cover the dog to keep it warm, and reassure it gently; it may become aggressive due to its injuries. Always use a muzzle on an injured pet; no matter how worried you are about your pet, human safety must come first.

CUT PADS

If your dog cuts the pads of its feet, they may bleed a lot as they have a rich blood supply. The most important first aid is to stop the bleeding. You can do this by applying firm pressure to the cut with a piece of cotton wool or gauze, or your fingers if you don't have anything else to hand. (You may wash the cut first, in saline solution.) You can then bandage the dressing firmly in place. A vet should take the dressing off because there may be more bleeding at this stage, and the cut may require stitching or treatment with antibiotics.

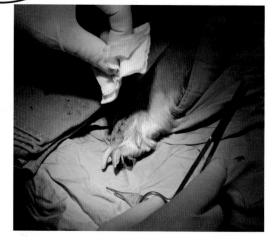

124

If your dog cuts its carpal pad (slightly up the foreleg), you will need to consult a vet immediately. This pad is close to an artery, and if this has been cut, it will need to be ligated (tied) to prevent further copious bleeding.

125

Never give an injured dog anything to eat or drink, as it may need an emergency anaesthetic.

CONVULSIONS

Seeing your dog have a convulsion can be frightening. The most important thing is to try to remain calm and prevent the dog from injuring itself. A convulsion may last between 30 seconds and two minutes; during this time, it may lose consciousness, foam at the mouth and urinate. Try to keep other people out of the room and darken it if possible. When the dog comes round, it will be disorientated and may act aggressively. You should consult a vet.

CARING FOR OLD DOGS

As dogs get older, they inevitably slow down and become susceptible to chronic illnesses or conditions such as cancer, kidney failure or blindness. They will need extra care and consideration to make their lives as comfortable and stress-free as possible. On the plus side, aging dogs tend to mellow out and become easier to live with.

AGE-RELATED PROBLEMS

Dogs often live longer now than they used to, due to vaccinations and medicines for all sorts of life-threatening diseases. However, eventually old age will catch up with even the healthiest dog. This can bring problems such as blindness – usually caused by cataracts – and deafness. Your dog may also slow down as arthritis begins to affect one or more joints. The liver, kidneys and heart may all start to fail, and cancer is common.

TREATMENT FOR OLDER DOGS

As with younger dogs, the best kind of treatment is prevention, so take your dog for a check-up by the vet every six months, and monitor its health yourself in between times. Tumours and cataracts can both be operated on in many cases, if they are caught early. Arthritis can't be cured, but the pain it causes can be managed with analgesic drugs.

126

Check older dogs regularly for any odd lumps or growths, which may indicate cancer, especially if they are accompanied by pain. If in doubt, get your dog checked by the vet.

SERIOUS OR CHRONIC ILLNESS

Dogs may be hospitalized for serious illnesses, but if you have the time and the knowledge, you may prefer to care for your sick dog at home. The dog may spend most if its time in bed, but encourage it to change position every so often to prevent sores and accumulation of fluid in the lungs, which may lead to pneumonia. Offer fresh water every hour (by syringe if necessary), and warm food. As the dog will not move much, keep it warm with a heat lamp or hot water bottle.

127

Old dogs' digestive systems cannot cope with large meals or rich food. Reduce the overall amount you feed your dog gradually, and consider giving two small meals a day rather than one large one.

128

Older dogs need shorter walks, but do give them plenty of opportunities to relieve themselves as they will need to urinate more frequently.

MEDICATING DOGS

Many kinds of illnesses and afflictions can cause your dog pain, and make it necessary for you to administer medication. It's important to recognize the signs of pain in your dog so that you can treat them. In the case of chronic pain especially, these signs may be subtle.

SIGNS OF PAIN

When your dog is in pain, it can't tell you in the way that another human would, so it's important to be sensitive to other signs. There are two types of pain – acute and chronic – and the signs that accompany each are different. Dogs in acute, sudden pain may be restless, with panting and shivering. They may growl and show signs of aggression, especially if you try to examine them; equally they may seem quiet and withdrawn. Dogs suffering from chronic, ongoing pain are likely to be reluctant to move (though in some cases, they may be reluctant to settle). Chronic pain can cause general depression and lethargy, and a simple change in behaviour may be the only sign.

PAINKILLERS

Most of the painkillers prescribed for dogs are non-steroidal anti-inflammatories. These are generally considered safe in the short and the long term. Acute pain may require a stronger treatment, and vets may prescribe morphine-type drugs. Sometimes dogs are prescribed aspirin – but always consult your vet before giving your dog any painkillers.

129

It may be tempting to try to hide tablets in your dog's food – but most pets soon see through this tactic and simply avoid eating them.

GIVING TABLETS

It may seem impossible to get your dog to swallow a tablet, but try the following method:
- Place one hand over the dog's muzzle and press the top lips inward with your finger.
- Take a tablet in your other hand and use the fingers of this hand to open the dog's mouth, pulling on the teeth of the lower jaw.
- Now hold the dog's mouth closed and stroke its throat. This should stimulate it to swallow the tablet.

130

Never give human medicines to dogs. The drugs themselves may be the same, but the dosages are likely to be very different. And some drugs taken by humans are entirely unsuitable for dogs.

TABLE OF SYMPTOMS

Use this table to check the possible causes of symptoms when your dog is sick. The best course of action is always to take your dog to the vet.

Symptom	Possible causes	Action
Abdominal distension (acute)	Gastric dilation, trauma, haemorrhage	This may be an emergency – take your dog to the vet immediately.
Abdominal distension (slowly increasing)	Pregnancy, constipation, enlarged organs, tumour, fluid in abdomen	Look for other signs, such as nipple enlargement or a cough. If symptoms persist, take your dog to the vet.
Alopecia (hair loss)	Demodex mites, hormone imbalance, excessive licking and scratching	Check for fleas. If symptoms persist, take your dog to the vet.
Appetite (increase, with weight gain)	Overfeeding, steroid therapy, metabolic disorder	Weigh the food ration daily and your dog weekly. Keep your dog under observation. If symptoms persist, take your dog to the vet.
Appetite (increase, with weight loss)	Diabetes, malabsorption, increased metabolic demands (e.g. due to pregnancy)	Observe the faeces and water intake. If symptoms persist, take your dog to the vet.
Appetite (loss of)	Fever, infection, pain, anxiety, hot weather, gastronintestinal disorder, organ failure	Keep your dog under observation and if symptoms persist take your dog to the vet.
Bad breath	Eating faeces, dental disease, oral infection	Check the dog's teeth and mouth; stop it from eating faeces, if this applies. Keep your dog under observation and if symptoms persist take your dog to the vet.
Bleeding from mouth	Trauma, infection	Look in the mouth. If symptoms persist, take your dog to the vet.
Bleeding from nose	Trauma, clotting disorder, persistent infection, tumour	Keep the nose down and place an ice pack on the muzzle. This may be an emergency – take your dog to the vet immediately.

Bleeding in faeces	Colitis, neoplasia	Keep your dog under observation. If symptoms persist, take your dog to the vet with a sample.
Bleeding in urine	Cystitis, stones, trauma, tumour	Take your dog to the vet if there is no improvement or if the condition worsens. Take a urine sample.
Bottom dragging along ground	Anal sacs full or infected	Check the area for soreness and fleas. If symptoms persist, take your dog to the vet.
Breathing (noisy)	Partial airway obstruction	This is a potentially fatal condition – the obstruction may shift. Take your dog to the vet immediately.
Breathing (rapid)	Haemorrhage, fear, respiratory disease, cardiac disease, metabolic disorder, brain disease	This may be an emergency – take your dog to the vet immediately. Try to remain calm to avoid upsetting your dog.
Chewing itself	Allergic skin disease, anal sacs full, fleas	Check for fleas. If symptoms persist, take your dog to the vet.
Constipation	Pain, poor food intake, bowel obstruction, muscle weakness	This may be an emergency – take your dog to the vet immediately.
Convulsions	Epilepsy, poisoning, metabolic problem, head trauma, tumour	This may be an emergency – take your dog to the vet immediately. Note the duration of the convulsion and any loss of consciousness.
Cough	Bronchitis, heart disease, infection, parasites such as heartworm	Keep your dog under observation. If symptoms persist, take your dog to the vet. Keep your dog away from others until the cause is known.
Diarrhoea	Infection, parasites, food intolerance, malabsorption, tumour, poison	Keep your dog under observation. If symptoms persist, take your dog to the vet. Note the frequency of defecation, the consistency of the faeces, and whether there is any blood.
Discharge from ear	Infection of outer ear canal	Clean the area carefully with a cotton ball, but take your dog to the vet. Cleaning alone will not clear up the condition.
Discharge from eye	Conjunctivitis	Wipe with sterile water. Keep your dog under observation for 24 to 48 hours. If symptoms persist, take your dog to the vet.

Discharge from nose	Foreign body, tumour, infection	Keep your dog under observation. If symptoms persist, take your dog to the vet. Note whether the discharge is from one or both nostrils.
Discharge from penis	Infection. Discharge may be normal in some dogs	Look for swelling. Keep your dog under observation. If symptoms persist, take your dog to the vet.
Discharge from vulva	Heat cycle, vaginitis, pyometra	Take your dog to the vet if there is no improvement or if the condition worsens – especially if the bitch has not been spayed and is not in heat.
Drinking excessively	Fever, kidney disease, diabetes, pyometra, adrenal gland disorder	Keep your dog under observation. If symptoms persist, take your dog to the vet. Measure water intake over 24 hours and collect a urine sample.
Ear held down	Infection, foreign body	Check ear for smell and discharge. Keep your dog under observation. If symptoms persist, take your dog to the vet.
Ear odour	Dirty ear, infection	Look in ear and note any redness or discharge. Keep your dog under observation. If symptoms persist, take your dog to the vet.
Ear scratching	Ear infection, foreign body, allergic skin disease	Check ear for discharge. Keep your dog under observation. If symptoms persist, take your dog to the vet.
Eye looks opaque	Corneal problem, cataract	Observe whether eye appears painful. Keep your dog under observation. If symptoms persist, take your dog to the vet.
Eye redness	Inflammation of conjunctiva, blood in eye	Keep your dog under observation. If symptoms persist, take your dog to the vet.
Eye semi-closed	Painful eye, foreign body, trauma, corneal ulcer, glaucoma	Bathe the area with sterile water. Take your dog to the vet immediately – certain conditions could result in the loss of an eye.
Eye – third eyelid up	Ocular problem or sign of general ill health	This may be an emergency – take your dog to the vet immediately.

Eye wet and runny	Irritation to eye	Check eye for obvious foreign bodies. Take your dog to the vet if there is no improvement or if the condition worsens.
Facial swelling	Allergic reaction to insect sting, abscess	This may be an emergency – take your dog to the vet immediately. Observe how quickly it develops.
Flatulence	Unsuitable diet, eating litter, old age	Keep your dog under observation. If symptoms persist, take your dog to the vet. Try changing the food and feed two to four times per day.
Gums bleed easily	Dental disease, infection, clotting disorder	Take your dog to the vet if there is no improvement, or if the condition worsens.
Gums sore	Gingivitis	Check the teeth. Keep your dog under observation. If symptoms persist, take your dog to the vet.
Head shaking	Foreign body, nasal irritation	This may be an emergency – take your dog to the vet immediately.
Head tilting	Disturbance of balance, ear or brain problem	Take your dog to the vet if there is no improvement, or if the condition worsens. Note if your dog is wobbly or circling.
Incontinence	Damage to nerves to bladder, urethral sphincter problem, prostate gland enlargement, excessive drinking	Keep your dog under observation. If symptoms persist, take your dog to the vet. Observe whether the problem is worse when the dog is standing or lying down and collect a urine sample.
Jaundice	Liver disease, tumour, anaemia, intravascular hemolysis, hepatitis	Take your dog to the vet immediately. Note the colour of the conjunctiva.
Lameness (front leg)	Developmental problems	Keep your dog under observation. If symptoms persist, take your dog to the vet. Strict rest.
Lameness (hind leg)	Hip dysplasia, patellar luxation	Keep your dog under observation. If symptoms persist, take your dog to the vet. Strict rest.
Lameness (painful and acute in any leg)	Sprain, fracture, dislocation, arthritis, bone tumour, developmental problems	This may be an emergency – take your dog to the vet immediately. Strict rest.

Lethargy	Heart disease, anaemia, hepatitis, renal diesease, among many other possible causes	If symptoms persist, take your dog to the vet.
Loss of consciousness	Head injury, epilepsy, faint, diabetic coma, intracranial haemorrhage	This may be an emergency – take your dog to the vet immediately. Keep the airway clear and make sure the dog is warm.
Lumps	Fatty lumps, warts, abscess, hernia, skin tumour	Feel for heat and pain. Keep your dog under observation. If symptoms persist, take your dog to the vet.
Mammary glands – lumps	Benign lumps, malignant tumours	Keep your dog under observation. If symptoms persist, take your dog to the vet.
Mouth – dribbling	Loose tooth, foreign body in mouth, infection, trauma	Look in the mouth, if possible. This may be an emergency – take your dog to the vet immediately.
Mouth – pawing at	Something stuck in mouth	Look in the mouth, if possible. This may be an emergency – take your dog to the vet immediately.
Nose – warm and dry	Fever, old age	Assess the general health. Keep your dog under observation. If symptoms persist, take your dog to the vet.
Panting	Fever, excitement, heatstroke, fear, hormonal disorder	Allow the dog to cool off and reassure it. Heatstroke is a medical emergency so take your dog to the vet immediately.
Regurgitation	Eating too fast, oesophagal obstruction, megaoesophagus	Try feeding smaller meals more frequently. Keep your dog under observation. If symptoms persist, take your dog to the vet.
Reluctance to exercise	Pain, cardiac disease, metabolic disease, heartworm	Keep your dog under observation. If symptoms persist, take your dog to the vet. Look for stiffness or other signs.
Salivation	Rabies, foreign body	Check mouth for wedged object. This may be an emergency – take your dog to the vet immediately.

Scratching	Fleas, mites, allergic skin disease	Look for fleas. Keep your dog under observation. If symptoms persist, take your dog to the vet.
Skin – scabby or spotty	Scratching, infection, mites, auto-immune skin disease	Keep your dog under observation. If symptoms persist, take your dog to the vet.
Skin – swelling	Abscess, lump	Feel for heat. Keep your dog under observation. If symptoms persist, take your dog to the vet.
Sneezing	Upper respiratory tract infection, nasal irritation	Look for nasal discharge. Keep your dog under observation. If symptoms persist, take your dog to the vet.
Squatting frequently	Cystitis, diabetes, pyometra, kidney disease	Obtain urine sample. Keep your dog under observation for 24 to 48 hours. If symptoms persist, take your dog to the vet.
Straining to defecate	Constipation, prostate gland enlargement, colitis, bowel obstruction	This may be an emergency – take your dog to the vet immediately.
Swallowing – difficulty	Trauma, tumours, pain	Check mouth and offer soft food. Keep your dog under observation. If symptoms persist, take your dog to the vet.
Temperature – raised	Infection, auto-immune disease, poison	Offer plenty of fresh water. Take your dog to the vet if there is no improvement or if the condition worsens.
Urination – excessive	Urinary tract infection, diabetes, kidney disease	Make plenty of water available. Keep your dog under observation. If symptoms persist, take your dog to the vet.
Vomiting	Gastrointestinal inflammation, obstruction, motion sickness, poisoning, dietary indiscretion	Take your dog to the vet if there is no improvement or if the condition worsens. Make a note of what your dog has eaten.
Weakness	Cardiac disease, metabolic problem, neurological disease, hormone disorder, old age	Keep your dog under observation. If symptoms persist, take your dog to the vet.
Weight gain	Overfeeding, inactivity, pregnancy, hormonal imbalance	Measure food intake. Keep your dog under observation. If symptoms persist, take your dog to the vet.
Weight loss	Inadequate quantity of food, difficulty eating, vomiting, impaired digestion and absorption	Feed two or three meals of high-energy food per day. Keep your dog under observation. If symptoms persist, take your dog to the vet.

9 PLANNING FOR EVERY EVENTUALITY

Once your dog is part of your life, you will need to take it into consideration when you are planning major events, such as moving house or going on holiday. Think about what will happen to your pet whether you decide to take it with you or need to leave it in kennels for a short period of time, or even rehome it if there are significant, long-term changes ahead.

Sadly, the time will also come when your dog dies, or you need to have it put down. You may not want to think about it, but there are, of course, practical considerations to take into account at this time, too.

HOLIDAYS

If you are planning a holiday, you will need to decide what to do with your dog. This is an issue, especially if you are planning overseas travel. The kinds of restrictions that govern whether you can take your dog with you will depend on where you live and where you are planning to travel.

TAKING YOUR DOG ABROAD

Some countries will allow pets to travel between them provided the dog has a pet passport. Getting a passport takes months, so you must plan in advance. The dog will need to be microchipped with information about its identity and ownership. Over a period of weeks, a vet will test the dog's blood and vaccinate it against rabies. The dog will need to be free of rabies and immune to the disease prior to being issued with a passport. Dogs being imported into a country may be quarantined if they have not been vaccinated or found free or infectious diseases and parasites prior to entry.

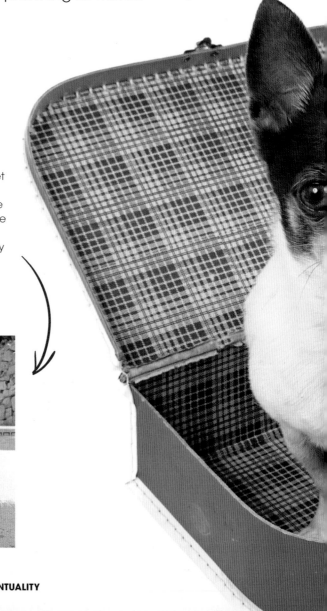

RABIES

Rabies is a deadly disease that affects mammals in some countries. It is spread when an infected animal bites another, and can be spread to humans in this way. Rabies in a person can often be prevented after a bite from an infected animal if anti-serum is given. However, this must be done before the symptoms of rabies develop (usually a few weeks after infection).

KENNELS

If you are going away on holiday, you may decide to put your dog in a kennel rather than take it with you. There are different kinds of kennels, and it's worth looking at the ones in your area to find one that seems suitable for your dog. Some kennels give each dog its own inside space and then let it run around outside every so often. Others are much more informal, and the dogs are kept in the kennel owner's home as if they were pets. You will need to prove that your dog's vaccinations are up-to-date, so take your documentation along. If you would like your dog to continue eating its usual food (best to avoid disruption to its diet), you will need to take a supply along to the kennel.

131

You may be able to find a friend or relative to "dog-sit" for you while you are away. The advantage is your dog can stick to its normal routine. Some companies also offer pet-sitting services, which may be useful if you have several animals.

REHOMING YOUR DOG

Sadly, you may find you need to rehome your dog. Think about this decision carefully because once you have handed the dog over to somebody else, you will not be able to get it back. Reasons for rehoming include changed circumstances due to family break-up or illness, or a change of job or location. Or, your dog may have behavioural problems that you simply cannot deal with yourself.

RETURNING THE DOG TO ITS BREEDER

If you bought your dog from a breeder, you may first try contacting them. A responsible breeder should agree to take back one of their own dogs at any point in the dog's life. (You should ask about this possibility when you first acquire the dog.)

PRIVATE SALE

You may decide to arrange a private sale or give your dog away. However, take care with this route, as once you hand over ownership, you will not be able to get your dog back. Do satisfy yourself that your dog is going to a loving, caring home, and not being sold into exploitation or poor living conditions.

RESCUE CENTRE

A third option is to take your dog to a rescue centre, which will rehome it for you. The quality of pet rescue centres varies, so visit a few and make sure that they rehome dogs responsibly. They should, at the least, interview potential new owners, and many also carry out home visits to ensure suitability. With this option, you may have to make a donation to the rescue centre in order for them to take your dog.

132

Be very sure of your decision to rehome your dog. It can't be reversed once you've done it.

PUTTING YOUR DOG TO SLEEP

It's not a decision you'll want to make, but it may become clear that you have to euthanize your dog (or "put it to sleep") if it is very old or ill and in pain, or if it has such serious behavioural problems that it is a danger to others. Often you will have time to make the decision (if your dog is in no immediate danger or pain), though sometimes the time will come quite unexpectedly, for example as the result of an accident.

THE PROCEDURE

If you decide the time has come to put your dog to sleep, the vet can perform the procedure for you. It is quite painless for the dog. The vet simply administers an anaesthetic injection from which the dog never wakes up. Once the dog has died, your vet can dispose of the remains, or you may opt to arrange your own burial or cremation.

BURIAL

If you decide to bury your dog, you have two options. You can bring the body home to bury yourself in your garden. Consider this carefully; if you are likely to be moving home in the near future, this may be inappropriate. If you do decide to bury your dog yourself, make the grave deep enough to keep it from being dug up by wild animals, which could obviously be very upsetting. Alternatively, you may decide to have your pet buried in a pet cemetery; this is a good option if you have no garden or are likely to move.

CREMATION

You may decide to have your dog cremated. Pets are cremated in the same way as humans, and you can choose to wait while the cremation takes place and then take the ashes away in an urn or box to dispose of as you wish.

GRIEVING

Your dog may have been with you for many years, and it is normal to feel upset and to grieve as you would for a person. You may find it helps to have your own simple service for your dog, and to plant a tree or erect a memorial to remember it. If you need to talk to someone about your feelings, there are telephone helplines and online forums you can turn to, if you feel you can't speak to your family or friends.

133

Remember that burial in a pet cemetery or cremation will cost a certain amount; this is unlikely to be covered by your pet insurance.

INDEX

INDEX

CREDITS